Editor
Erica N. Russikoff, M.A.

Editor in Chief
Karen J. Goldfluss, M.S. Ed.

Cover Artist
Tony Carrillo
Brenda DiAntonis

Imaging
James Edward Grace
Craig Gunnell

Publisher
Mary D. Smith, M.S. Ed.

TCR 5035

DAILY W

Nonfiction Reading Grade 5

CORRELATED TO COMMON CORE STANDARDS

Includes:

- ▶ 150 leveled passages with a variety of interesting topics
- ▶ Comprehension questions that target reading skills & strategies
- ▶ Standards & Benchmarks

Ideal for test preparation

30 passages & activities in each of these sections:
Interesting Places & Events
Scientifically Speaking
From the Past
Did You Know?
Fascinating People

Teacher Created Resources

Author
Ruth Foster, M. Ed.

CORRELATED TO COMMON CORE STANDARDS

Correlations to the Common Core State Standards can be found at *http://www.teachercreated.com/standards/*.

The classroom teacher may reproduce the materials in this book and/or CD for use in a single classroom only. The reproduction of any part of this book and/or CD for other classrooms or for an entire school or school system is strictly prohibited. No part of this publication may be transmitted or recorded in any form without written permission from the publisher with the exception of electronic material, which may be stored on the purchaser's computer only.

Teacher Created Resources
6421 Industry Way
Westminster, CA 92683
www.teachercreated.com

ISBN: 978-1-4206-5035-8

©*2011 Teacher Created Resources*
Reprinted, 2014
Made in U.S.A.

Teacher Created Resources

Table of Contents

Table of Contents (cont.)

Introduction

The primary goal of any reading task is comprehension. *Daily Warm-Ups: Nonfiction Reading* uses high-interest, grade-level appropriate nonfiction passages followed by assessment practice to help develop confident readers who can demonstrate their skills on standardized tests. Each passage is a high-interest nonfiction text that fits one of the five topic areas: Interesting Places and Events, Scientifically Speaking, From the Past, Did You Know?, and Fascinating People. Each of these five topic areas has 30 passages, for a total of 150 passages. Each passage, as well as its corresponding multiple-choice assessment questions, is provided on one page.

Comprehension Questions

The questions in *Daily Warm-Ups: Nonfiction Reading* assess all levels of comprehension, from basic recall to critical thinking. The questions are based on fundamental reading skills found in scope-and-sequence charts across the nation:

- recall information
- use prior knowledge
- visualize
- recognize the main idea
- identify supporting details
- understand cause and effect

- sequence in chronological order
- identify synonyms and antonyms
- know grade-level vocabulary
- use context clues to understand new words
- make inferences
- draw conclusions

Readability

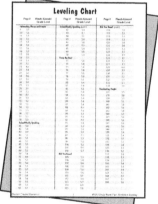

The texts have a 5.0–6.0 grade level based on the Flesch-Kincaid Readability Formula. This formula, built into Microsoft Word®, determines readability by calculating the number of words, syllables, and sentences. Multisyllabic words tend to skew the grade level, making it appear higher than it actually is. Refer to the Leveling Chart on page 175 for the approximate grade level of each passage.

Including Standards and Benchmarks

The passages and comprehension questions throughout this book correlate with McREL (Mid-Continent Research for Education and Learning) Standards. Known as a "Compendium of Standards and Benchmarks," this resource is well researched. It includes standards and benchmarks that represent a consolidation of national and state standards in several content areas for grades K–12. (See page 6 for the specific McREL Standards and Benchmarks that correspond with this book.) These standards have been aligned to the Common Core State Standards. To view them, please visit *http://www.teachercreated.com/standards/*.

Practice First to Build Familiarity

Initial group practice is essential. Read aloud the first passage in each of the five topic areas and do its related questions with the whole class. Depending upon the needs of your class, you may choose to do the first three passages in each topic area as a whole class. Some teachers like to use five days in a row to model the reading and question-answering process at the start of the year. Model pre-reading the questions, reading the text, highlighting information that refers to the comprehension questions, and eliminating answers that are obviously incorrect. You may also want to model referring back to the text to ensure the answers selected are the best ones.

Introduction *(cont.)*

Student Practice Ideas

With *Daily Warm-Ups: Nonfiction Reading* you can choose to do whole-class or independent practice. For example, you can use the passages and questions for the following:

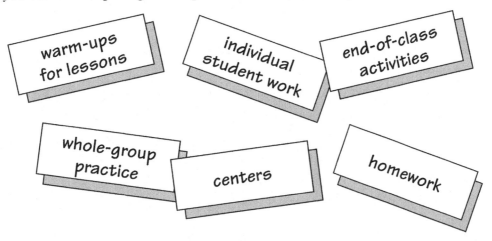

Whichever method you choose for using the book, it's a good idea to practice as a class how to read a passage and respond to the comprehension questions. In this way, you can demonstrate your own thought processes by "thinking aloud" to figure out an answer. Essentially, this means that you tell your students your thoughts as they come to you.

Self-Monitoring Reading Strategies

Use the reading strategies on page 174 with your students so they can monitor their own reading comprehension. Copy and distribute this page to your students, or turn it into a class poster. Have your students use these steps for this text, as well as future texts.

Record Keeping

In the sun image at the bottom, right-hand corner of each warm-up page, there is a place for you (or for students) to write the number of questions answered correctly. This will give consistency to scored pages. Use the Tracking Sheet on page 176 to record which warm-up exercises you have given to your students. Or distribute copies of the sheet for students to keep their own records.

How to Make the Most of This Book

- ✏ Read each lesson ahead of time before you use it with the class so that you are familiar with it. This will make it easier to answer students' questions.

- ✏ Set aside ten to twelve minutes at a specific time daily to incorporate *Daily Warm-Ups: Nonfiction Reading* into your routine.

- ✏ Make sure the time you spend working on the materials is positive and constructive. This should be a time of practicing for success and recognizing it as it is achieved.

The passages and comprehension questions in *Daily Warm-Ups: Nonfiction Reading* are time-efficient, allowing your students to practice these skills often. The more your students practice reading and responding to content-area comprehension questions, the more confident and competent they will become.

Standards and Benchmarks

Each passage in *Daily Warm-Ups: Nonfiction Reading* meets at least one of the following standards and benchmarks, which are used with permission from McREL. Copyright 2010 McREL. Mid-continent Research for Education and Learning. 4601 DTC Boulevard, Suite 500, Denver, CO 80237. Telephone: 303-337-0990. Web site: *www.mcrel.org/standards-benchmarks*. Correlations to the Common Core State Standards can be found at *http://www.teachercreated.com/standards/*.

Uses the general skills and strategies of the reading process

- Establishes a purpose for reading
- Makes, confirms, and revises simple predictions about what will be found in a text
- Uses phonetic and structural analysis techniques, syntactic structure, and semantic context to decode unknown words
- Uses a variety of context clues to decode unknown words
- Understands level-appropriate reading vocabulary
- Monitors own reading strategies and makes modifications as needed
- Understands the author's purpose

Uses skills and strategies to read a variety of literary texts

- Reads a variety of literary passages and texts

Uses skills and strategies to read a variety of informational texts

- Reads a variety of informational texts
- Uses text organizers to determine the main ideas and to locate information in a text
- Summarizes and paraphrases information in texts
- Uses prior knowledge and experience to understand and respond to new information
- Understands structural patterns or organization in informational texts

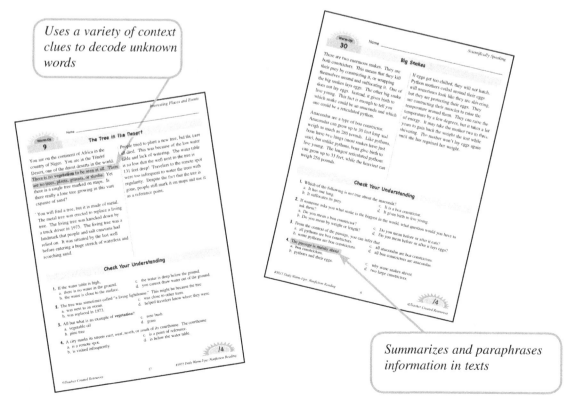

Uses a variety of context clues to decode unknown words

Summarizes and paraphrases information in texts

Interesting Places and Events

Warm-Up

1

Name _____

Mystery of the Rolling Stones

Death Valley is a desert that is located in California. Death Valley is known for its climate. It is the hottest place in the United States. It is also known for its elevation. It has the lowest elevation in North America. It is 282 feet below sea level. Death Valley is also known for a mystery. The mystery has to do with rolling stones.

The rolling rocks are found on a dry lakebed. The lakebed is called Racetrack Playa. The dry lakebed is scattered with stones of varying sizes. Some stones are fist-sized, while others are as big as a picnic cooler and weigh more than 660 pounds.

The mystery about the stones is that they move. No one has seen the stones move, but people can see where the stones have rolled by the trails gouged into the ground behind them.

Scientists studied the rocks. They took GPS (Global Positioning System) measurements of the rocks. Scientists measured them before they moved and after. What is the answer to the mystery behind the moving rocks? One theory is that sometimes the lakebed gets slick with mud after a heavy rainfall. Then strong winds blow the rocks across the slippery surface.

Check Your Understanding

1. Which of the following is *not* true about Death Valley?
   a. It is a desert.
   b. It never rains in Death Valley.
   c. It is the lowest point in North America.
   d. It is the hottest place in the United States.

2. How did people know the rocks had moved before scientists took GPS measurements?
   a. There was heavy rainfall.
   b. There were strong winds blowing.
   c. There was slick mud on the lakebed.
   d. There were trails gouged into the ground.

3. The passage is mainly about
   a. some rocks in Death Valley.
   b. mysteries in North America.
   c. big stones around the world.
   d. heavy rainfall in California.

4. Which of the following items vary in size?
   a. pencils in a package
   b. tennis balls in a can
   c. shoes in a shoe store
   d. eggs in an egg carton

/4

Warm-Up 2

Name _____

A Misnamed Ocean

The Pacific Ocean is the world's largest body of water. It covers 28 percent of the global surface. This is more than the total land area of the world. The Pacific contains the deepest ocean trenches in the world. Its deepest trench is the Mariana Trench. At its deepest point, this trench is deeper than Mount Everest is high. The Pacific has over 25,000 islands. This is more than all the other oceans combined. It contains large islands like Japan and Taiwan. It also contains islands that are too small to be named. Most of its islands are south of the equator.

The Pacific Ocean was named by Ferdinand Magellan. Magellan was an explorer from Portugal. He named the ocean in 1520. He named it after the word "pacifico," which means peaceful. Magellan thought that the Pacific's winds and climate were gentler than the other oceans. He was wrong.

The Pacific is actually the most violent of the oceans. Large storms spring up near the equator. The storms have high winds that rage across the water. It also has a "Ring of Fire." This ring contains nearly three hundred active volcanoes. Waves caused by earthquakes are called *tsunamis*. Because of its depth, Pacific tsunamis can reach extremely fast speeds. Some tsunamis move as fast as a jet plane!

Check Your Understanding

1. Which of the following is *not* true about the Pacific Ocean?
   a. It is the deepest ocean.
   b. It is the warmest ocean.
   c. It is the largest ocean.
   d. It contains the most islands.

2. Magellan was an explorer from
   a. Spain.
   b. France.
   c. Portugal.
   d. Great Britain.

3. *Pacific* is the name of an ocean, but it is also an adjective. Most likely, a *pacific day* is
   a. stormy and cold.
   b. rainy and windy.
   c. wild and reckless.
   d. calm and peaceful.

4. From the context of the passage, you can infer that when Magellan first saw the Pacific Ocean,
   a. it was a beautiful day.
   b. he was by a large island.
   c. a tsunami was going at an incredibly fast speed.
   d. he went to the bottom of the Mariana Trench.

/4

Warm-Up 3

Name _____

Tet

People in the United States use a calendar when the new year starts on January 1, but not every country is the same. Vietnam is a country in Southeast Asia. The Vietnamese New Year is called *Tet*. *Tet* occurs in late January or February. The break between years falls between the harvesting of crops and the sowing of new crops.

The Vietnamese get ready for *Tet* well in advance. They clean their houses. They polish silverware and copper items. They pay off debts. Special foods are eaten on *Tet*. One special food is a rice pudding that contains mung beans and pork. Watermelon is eaten because its red color is thought to be lucky. On New Year's Day, children are given lucky red envelopes. The envelopes contain money.

The first visitor outside the family on New Year's Day is very important. It is believed that the first person through the door will influence the family's luck, happiness, and wealth for the coming year. For example, if a rich person enters, the family's fortune will increase. If a cheerful person enters, the family will experience joy. What do some people do to insure that the year goes well? They carefully choose their first guest!

Check Your Understanding

1. If you are picking out a watermelon for *Tet*, you want the
   a. biggest and ripest one.
   b. the one with the least seeds.
   c. the cheapest and heaviest one.
   d. the one with the reddest flesh.

2. Another title for the passage might be
   a. "Lucky Colors."
   b. "What's in the Envelope?"
   c. "When the First Guest Matters."
   d. "The First of January in Vietnam."

3. The special pudding contains all but
   a. corn.
   b. rice.
   c. pork.
   d. beans.

4. From the context of the passage, you can infer that the New Year date
   a. always falls on the same day.
   b. depends on what country you are in.
   c. always has to do with harvesting crops.
   d. depends on how happy or wealthy you are.

/4

Warm-Up
4

Name _____

A Massive Structure

A scientist was using satellite imagery. He was tracking melting permafrost in Canada's far North when he accidentally found an enormous structure. It was about 2,800 feet long. It was so big that it could be seen from space. The structure had not been made by people. What was the structure? Who had made it? When was it constructed?

The structure was a massive beaver dam. Discovered in 2007, scientists believe it is the **largest** beaver dam on record, and it is still growing! Scientists believe construction started in the 1970s. Several generations of beavers have worked on the dam. The dam is located in Wood Buffalo Park in northern Alberta. It is a remote area that is very hard to get to. When the dam was discovered by satellite imagery, rangers flew over the area in a plane to take a look at it.

How did the rangers date the dam? They looked at the grasses and other vegetation growing on the logs. A new dam would have fresh sticks. Parts of this dam were covered with green growth. A beaver can gnaw down a tree in a few hours, and it can fell two hundred trees in a year.

Check Your Understanding

1. Most likely, the author did *not* tell you what the structure was in the title because she wanted
a. to make you curious.
b. to make you feel afraid.
c. to make you lose interest.
d. to make sure there were no surprises.

2. When did you finally learn what the massive structure was?
a. at the very beginning
b. in the first paragraph
c. in the third paragraph
d. in the second paragraph

3. Which of the following words is *not* a synonym for **largest**?
a. big
b. fresh
c. massive
d. enormous

4. From the context of the passage, you can infer that rangers used a plane to look at the dam because
a. green growth covered the dam.
b. the dam was discovered by accident.
c. the dam was remote and hard to get to.
d. several generations had worked on the dam.

/4

Warm-Up

Name _____

5   The Legend of Lady Carcas

Carcassonne is an ancient city in France located on a rocky hilltop. It is fortified by high, surrounding walls. The stone walls are sixteen to twenty-three feet high and more than ten feet thick. The city was attacked in the eighth century. There is a famous legend about how the city successfully defended itself.

Prince Balaach, the ruler of the city, was killed in one of the early attacks. His widow, Lady Carcas, **donned** his armor and took up the fight. After five long years, there was hardly anyone left to defend the city, and the people were beginning to starve. Instead of giving up, Lady Carcas made straw manikins. Then she placed the manikins around the walls, so it looked like she still had plenty of soldiers.

Next, she found the biggest pig she could find. Before throwing the pig over the wall, she stuffed it full of hay so it looked well fed.

The people attacking the city were astonished. They had thought they could starve the people out, but if people could get rid of such a fat pig, they must have plenty of food. The attackers gave up. Lady Carcas blew her horn in victory. The city was named when a warrior called out, "Carcas sonne," meaning Carcas was blowing her horn.

Check Your Understanding

1. If you went to Carcassonne today, you could
   a. see Lady Carcas.
   b. see the manikins.
   c. see the stuffed pig.
   d. see the fortifying walls.

2. The passage is mainly about
   a. ancient fighting tricks.
   b. life in the eighth century.
   c. Prince Balaach and his wife.
   d. the legend behind a city's name.

3. When Lady Carcas **donned** her husband's armor,
   a. she hid it.
   b. she wore it.
   c. she burned it.
   d. she stuffed it.

4. Which of the following statements do you know to be false?
   a. Lady Carcas stuffed a pig.
   b. Lady Carcas made straw manikins.
   c. The city was attacked in the eighth century.
   d. The city is located in a grassy valley in France.

/4

Name _____

No International Postage

When you mail a letter, there are different rates. The rates are determined by weight, carrier, and destination. For example, mail carried by airplane is more expensive than that sent by rail, ship, or van. There are domestic rates. There are international rates. Domestic rates are cheaper. Domestic mail is within the United States. International rates are higher. Mail sent to other countries costs more.

Guam is a tropical island. It has its own flag. Located in the western Pacific Ocean, Guam is the largest and southernmost of the Mariana Islands. Guam is far from the U.S. mainland. In fact, it is in a different hemisphere. The continental U.S. is in the Western Hemisphere. Guam is in the Eastern Hemisphere.

Guam may be a distant island, but domestic mail rates apply! You pay the same as if you sent a letter from one end of town to another. This is because Guam is a U.S. territory. The U.S. has other territories, too. Puerto Rico and the U.S. Virgin Islands are U.S. territories. They are both located in the Caribbean. American Samoa and the Northern Mariana Islands are also territories. They are both located in the Pacific. These places may be spread across the world, but to the U.S. postal service, they are all domestic!

Check Your Understanding

1. What two hemispheres could Guam be in?
 a. northern and eastern
 b. northern and western
 c. southern and western
 d. southern and northern

2. From the context of the passage, you can infer that, most likely,
 a. Puerto Rico has its own flag.
 b. Puerto Rico doesn't have a flag.
 c. Puerto Rico has the same flag as Guam.
 d. Puerto Rico has the same flag as American Samoa.

3. The passage is mainly about
 a. why airmail costs more.
 b. sending international mail.
 c. where domestic postal rates apply.
 d. how many cents it costs to send a letter.

4. To mail a letter, which of the following pairs of locations would require you to pay international postal rates?
 a. Maine to American Samoa
 b. California to Australia
 c. Idaho to Northern Mariana Islands
 d. Rhode Island to U.S. Virgin Islands

/4

Name _____

Where the Unicorn Lives

There is a place described as "where the unicorn lives." The unicorn is a mythical creature with one horn. Does this mythical creature exist? If so, where does it live?

The Arabian Oryx is a medium-sized antelope. It is well adapted to desert life. It has white fur and black skin. The white fur reflects the heat of the bright sun. The black skin helps protect it from the sun's ultraviolet rays and from getting sunburnt. Its most striking feature is its horns. Its sharp horns curve slightly backward. They can measure up to thirty-five inches in length. The horns are perfectly symmetrical. In fact, the horns are so evenly balanced that if you look at the Oryx in profile, or sideways, it looks like the Oryx has only one horn.

The Arabian Oryx lives in Oman. Oman is in Asia. It is on the southeast coast of the Arabian Peninsula. The wild Oryx was hunted to extinction in 1972. Fortunately, a few captive animals were donated to start a breeding program. This made it possible to bring a small herd back to Oman in 1980. A sanctuary, or nature reserve, was set up in Oman for the Oryx. It is called the Arabian Oryx Sanctuary. The reserve is located within the central desert and coastal hills.

Check Your Understanding

1. Most likely, the Oryx is sometimes called a unicorn because
   a. it is a mythical creature.
   b. it can look like it has only one horn.
   c. it lives in a sanctuary in the desert.
   d. it was hunted to extinction in the wild.

2. Oman is on the
   a. northeast coast of the Arabian Peninsula.
   b. southeast coast of the Arabian Peninsula.
   c. northwest coast of the Arabian Peninsula.
   d. southwest coast of the Arabian Peninsula.

3. From the context of the passage, you can infer that the Oryx
   a. lives in Asia.
   b. needs lots of water.
   c. cannot breed in captivity.
   d. is larger than most antelopes.

4. Which letter, if folded in half, has two symmetrical halves?
   a. O
   b. R
   c. P
   d. L

/4

Name _____

The Forbidden City

The Forbidden City is a palace where the emperor of China once lived. Commoners could not enter. It was built between 1406 and 1420, and it is located in the center of Beijing. Today, it is known as the Palace Museum. It is surrounded by a wall and made up of buildings and courtyards. There are over 9,000 rooms. If the emperor slept in a different room every night, he would be over twenty-four and one-half years old before he could sleep in the same room twice!

There are over three hundred large bronze vats, or pots, throughout the palace. The vats were filled with water. Sometimes, the vats were lined and covered with blankets. Sometimes, fires were lit beneath them. The vats were for decoration, but what else were they for? They were filled with water in case of a fire! The blankets and fires were so the water wouldn't freeze in the winter.

The palace was constructed with slabs of marble, huge rocks, and wood from heavy logs. How were the construction materials brought to the palace site? They were brought during the winter. Water was splashed onto the road, turning it into a sheet of ice. The materials, loaded onto sleds, were then pulled and pushed on the slippery surface.

Check Your Understanding

1. Most likely, the palace was called "The Forbidden City" because
a. commoners could not enter.
b. it is surrounded by a wall.
c. the emperor once lived there.
d. it is in the center of Beijing.

2. Another title for the passage might be
a. "Safe from Fire."
b. "Chinese Palaces."
c. "The Palace Museum."
d. "The Emperor of China."

3. The emperor usually didn't sleep in every room. The author told you how long it would have taken the emperor if he had so you could get a picture of
a. just how many rooms 6,000 is.
b. just how many rooms 7,000 is.
c. just how many rooms 8,000 is.
d. just how many rooms 9,000 is.

4. What would you expect a winter in Beijing to be like?
a. windy and fresh
b. cold and snowy
c. sunny and warm
d. chilly and misty

/4

Warm-Up
9

Name _____

The Tree in the Desert

You are on the continent of Africa in the country of Niger. You are in the Ténéré Desert, one of the driest deserts in the world. There is no **vegetation** to be seen at all. There are no trees, plants, grasses, or shrubs. Yet there is a single tree marked on maps. Is there really a lone tree growing in this vast expanse of sand?

You will find a tree, but it is made of metal. The metal tree was erected to replace a living tree. The living tree was knocked down by a truck driver in 1973. The living tree was a landmark that people and salt caravans had relied on. It was situated by the last well before entering a huge stretch of waterless and scorching sand.

People tried to plant a new tree, but the trees all died. This was because of the low water table and lack of watering. The water table is so low that the well next to the tree is 131 feet deep! Travelers to the remote spot were too infrequent to water the trees with regularity. Despite the fact that the tree is gone, people still mark it on maps and use it as a reference point.

Check Your Understanding

1. If the water table is high,
   a. there is no water in the ground.
   b. the water is close to the surface.
   c. the water is deep below the ground.
   d. you cannot draw water out of the ground.

2. The tree was sometimes called "a living lighthouse" because the tree
   a. was next to an ocean.
   b. was replaced in 1973.
   c. was close to other trees.
   d. helped travelers know where they were.

3. All but what is an example of **vegetation**?
   a. vegetable oil
   b. pine tree
   c. rose bush
   d. grass

4. A city marks its streets *east*, *west*, *north*, or *south* of its courthouse. The courthouse
   a. is a remote spot.
   b. is visited infrequently.
   c. is a point of reference.
   d. is below the water table.

/4

Warm-Up 10

Name _____

The Ice Bowl

It was a game where the officials could not use their whistles. They had to shout to call plays dead. It was the last day of 1967, and the Dallas Cowboys were playing against the Green Bay Packers in Green Bay, Wisconsin. Whoever won the game would be the National Football League champions. Whoever won the game would go on to play in the Super Bowl.

At the beginning of the game, the officials had tried to use their whistles. They had to stop after one of the referee's whistles froze to his lips! The Cowboys' coach said, "It was like being at the North Pole." It was so cold that temperatures **plummeted** down to 13°F below zero. With the wind chill factor, it felt like it was 48°F below.

Players from both teams were slipping on the icy turf. Both sides had to adjust to the playing conditions. Finally, it was the Packers who won out. They won because quarterback Bart Starr called a play called a "quarterback sneak." It was a risky call, but Starr was confident he could pull it off. Despite Starr's stellar performance, people once believed he could not be a successful quarterback. In college, he barely played. When he was drafted, he was the 17th round pick, and even then he was almost dropped from the roster.

Check Your Understanding

1. From the context of the passage, you can infer that the fans in the stands were wearing
   a. tee shirts.
   b. heavy coats.
   c. sweatshirts.
   d. light jackets.

2. If the passage was longer, the next paragraph might go on to talk about
   a. what referees do.
   b. what a wind chill factor is.
   c. what Starr did to become a stellar quarterback.
   d. what all the teams in the National Football League are like.

3. On what day of the year was the game played?
   a. January 1
   b. January 30
   c. December 30
   d. December 31

4. When temperatures **plummet**, they
   a. drop down.
   b. begin to rise.
   c. stay the same.
   d. go down just a little.

/4

Warm-Up

11

Name _____

No Need to Build

Oftentimes, moviemakers need to build sets. The sets are the background for the movie scenes. Sometimes, moviemakers don't need to build a set. They may find a house or a location that they can rent or use for free. *Star Wars* is a film series that takes place in the future. Despite its futuristic setting, some of the scenes from the first movie were filmed in houses that were hundreds of years old!

The houses were troglodyte dwellings. They were located in Tunisia. Tunisia is a desert country in northern Africa. Troglodyte dwellings are in caves or under the ground. The troglodyte homes used in the film were in the small village of Matmata. They were built in ancient times, but people still live in them today.

The houses were first constructed by digging a large pit, about 16 to 33 feet deep in the ground. Next, caves were dug out around the perimeter of the pit. The caves were used as rooms for sleeping, grain storage, and family gatherings. Storage nooks for food and shelves were cut directly into walls, and the rooms were connected by narrow passageways. Access to a home was through a sloping tunnel or by a ladder.

Check Your Understanding

1. Tunisia is a country in
   a. eastern Africa.
   b. western Africa.
   c. southern Africa.
   d. northern Africa.

2. A troglodyte lives in a cave or under the ground. What animal could be called a troglodyte?
   a. bat
   b. deer
   c. tiger
   d. eagle

3. Which of the following statements is true about movie sets?
   a. No movie sets are rented.
   b. All movie sets are rented.
   c. Most movie sets are rented.
   d. Some movie sets are rented.

4. The passage is mainly about
   a. a movie set.
   b. building movie sets.
   c. making ancient movies.
   d. people who live in caves.

/4

Warm-Up
12

Name _____

Needed: Hot and Cold Hands

A man sits down to make a sculpture. Over and over, the man dips his hands into buckets of hot and cold water. He may do this for months. What kind of sculpture is the artist making, and why does he need to repeatedly dip his hands?

The man is making a sculpture out of butter for a New Year celebration ceremony in Tibet. This ceremony takes place on the 15th day of the Tibetan New Year (sometime in January through March). The butter is made from yak milk. Domesticated yaks are large, long-haired herd animals that are kept for their milk, meat, and hair. They are also kept for their dung, which is used as fuel. A butter sculpture may be a god or a flower. It may be a panel that depicts characters and scenes.

It is made to honor Buddha. Some are quite large and take months of detailed work.

Butter melts, so the artist's hands must be cold when he works. Butter is sticky, too, so the artist's hands must be clean. Over and over, the artist has to wash his hands to clean them in the hot water, and then he has to cool them in the cold water before he picks up some more butter. Despite the months spent preparing the sculptures, they are dismantled as soon as the ceremony ends.

Check Your Understanding

1. *Domesticated* is to *wild* as
   a. *ended* is to *over*.
   b. *picked* is to *chosen*.
   c. *warmed* is to *heated*.
   d. *dismantled* is to *build*.

2. For what are the butter sculptures used?
   a. eating
   b. fuel
   c. cleaning
   d. honoring Buddha

3. The butter ceremony may take place on
   a. June 25.
   b. April 15.
   c. February 5.
   d. December 30.

4. Another title for the passage might be
   a. "New Year Butter Sculptures."
   b. "Celebrations in Tibet."
   c. "How Artists Keep Clean."
   d. "New Year Around the World."

/4

Name _____

13   The Race Across the Sky

Think of a very long race. Did you think of a marathon? A marathon is a bit over twenty-six miles. The "Race Across the Sky" is more than a marathon. It is an ultramarathon. How long is this ultramarathon? It is one hundred miles! Its name comes from the high altitude at which it is run.

Held **annually**, the ultramarathon is run on dirt trails and dirt roads out of Leadville, Colorado. Leadville is a city in the Rocky Mountains. Leadville was a booming silver-mining camp in the 1880s. Today, it is the highest incorporated city in the United States.

The racecourse is extremely difficult, which is just one of the reasons why it's only run once a year. Runners run at elevations ranging between 9,200 and 12,620 feet. During the run, they climb and descend one high mountain pass twice. The race starts at 4:00 a.m. There is a thirty-hour time limit. There are eleven aid stations. There are five medical checkpoints at the aid stations. Runners must leave the race if they miss a medical checkpoint deadline. Many runners don't finish. In 2005, one forty-one-year-old man surprised everyone. How did he surprise everyone? He finished in daylight! He ran the race in only fifteen hours and forty-two minutes.

Check Your Understanding

1. The race starts
   a. late in the morning.
   b. late in the evening.
   c. early in the morning.
   d. early in the evening.

2. Another title for the passage might be
   a. "More Than a Marathon."
   b. "Mining in the Mountains."
   c. "From Checkpoint to Checkpoint."
   d. "The Highest City in the World."

3. When something happens **annually**, it happens
   a. once a year.
   b. once a month.
   c. once a decade.
   d. once a century.

4. Which of the following is *not* true about Leadville?
   a. It is in Colorado.
   b. It is in the Rocky Mountains.
   c. It was once a gold-mining camp.
   d. It is the highest incorporated city in the United States.

/4

Warm-Up
14

Name _____

The Giant's Causeway

The Giant's **Causeway** is in Northern Ireland. It is an area of 40,000 interlocking columns. The columns are a result of a volcanic eruption that took place sixty million years ago. The columns are basalt. Basalt is a kind of volcanic rock. Most of the columns are hexagonal, but some have four, five, seven, or eight sides instead of six. The tops of the columns form stepping stones that lead into the sea.

There is a legend about this rock formation. The legend is about two giants. One giant lived in Ireland. The other lived in Scotland across the sea. The Irish giant built a causeway so he could fight the Scottish giant.

The Irish giant crossed over, but then he saw how big the Scottish giant was. The Irish giant ran back home. He devised a plan.

The Irish giant had his wife cover him with a blanket. When the Scottish giant came looking for him, the Irish giant's wife pretended that it was her baby under the blanket. The Scottish giant fled in terror because he thought, "If the baby is so big, the father must be a monster!" As the Scottish giant fled, he ripped up the causeway so he couldn't be followed.

Check Your Understanding

1. How many sides does a hexagon have?
   a. five
   b. six
   c. seven
   d. eight

2. A **causeway** is another word for
   a. a tunnel under the water.
   b. a bridge made out of wood.
   c. a street with a traffic light.
   d. a raised road across wet ground.

3. What did the Irish giant do to the Scottish giant?
   a. He fought him.
   b. He killed him.
   c. He tricked him.
   d. He laughed at him.

4. The passage is mainly about
   a. what basalt is.
   b. volcanic eruptions.
   c. a giant who lived in Scotland.
   d. a legend about a rock formation.

/4

Warm-Up 15

Name _____

So Just Where Are You?

You're not sure of your exact location. You look out the window, and you see a road with road signs written in English. Suddenly, you see a car going down the road. You know at once that you are in England, not the United States.

You're not sure of your exact location. You look out the window, and you see a world of snow and ice. Suddenly, you see some penguins. You know at once that you are in Antarctica, not the Arctic.

You're not sure of your exact location. You look out the window and spot an alligator or a crocodile. Suddenly, you get a good look at the huge creature's wide, rounded, U-shaped snout. You know at once that you are in North America, not Africa.

How did you know which one of the two choices was your location? Cars in England and the United States drive on opposite sides of the road. In England, cars drive on the left, while in the United States, they drive on the right. Penguins only live in the Southern Hemisphere, so they can't live in the Arctic. Alligators have wide, rounded, U-shaped snouts, and they don't live in Africa. African-dwelling crocodiles have longer, pointed, V-shaped snouts.

Check Your Understanding

1. You are in Australia. You see a crocodile. You know it is a crocodile because
   a. it has a V-shaped snout.
   b. it has an I-shaped snout.
   c. it has a T-shaped snout.
   d. it has a U-shaped snout.

2. From the context of the passage, you can infer that the Arctic is in
   a. the Eastern Hemisphere.
   b. the Western Hemisphere.
   c. the Northern Hemisphere.
   d. the Southern Hemisphere.

3. A car is being driven on the left-hand side of the road. From the context of the passage, you can infer that the car is *not* being driven in
   a. Australia.
   b. the United States.
   c. the Solomon Islands.
   d. the British Virgin Islands.

4. Most likely, cars in England and the United States
   a. are exactly the same.
   b. do not have spare tires.
   c. have steering wheels on opposite sides.
   d. can't be driven on roads without signs.

/4

Warm-Up 16

Name _____

Back on the Map

A city in the Southern Hemisphere was built on the top of a high mountain. The city was made with huge blocks of stone. The blocks of stone fit together so well that it was impossible to slide a piece of paper between them. The stone buildings were carefully positioned and built to line up with certain points. One building was aligned so that the sun shone through its windows on the summer solstice. The summer solstice is the longest day of the year. The ground around the buildings was carefully terraced. The city was put back on the map after 400 years. How can a city be lost?

The city, located in Peru, is known as Machu Picchu. It was built by the Incas around 1450.

It was abandoned about 100 years later. It was "lost" because of its high elevation and remote location. Yet its location may also be what saved it. It was too far away from everything else for the Spanish to find. It was safe from the greedy conquistadores who were looting for gold.

Machu Picchu wasn't put back on the map until 1911. That was when local peasants showed the ruins to Hiram Bingham. Bingham was an archeologist. Today, the city is a well-known tourist spot.

Check Your Understanding

1. About what year was Machu Picchu abandoned by the Incas?
a. 1350
b. 1450
c. 1550
d. 1650

2. Which of the following words means "far away or distant"?
a. greedy
b. remote
c. terraced
d. solstice

3. Another title for the passage might be
a. "An Ancient City in Asia."
b. "An Ancient City in Europe."
c. "An Ancient City in South America."
d. "An Ancient City in North America."

4. Which of the following is true about Machu Picchu?
a. It was built by the Spanish.
b. It is at a high elevation in Peru.
c. It was put back on the map in 1811.
d. It was looted by the conquistadores.

/4

Warm-Up
17

Name _____

The Case of the Poisoned Tiger

There was a mystery at the Windsor Safari Park (known today as LEGOLAND Windsor). The park was on the outskirts of Windsor in Berkshire, England. Zelda the tiger had been poisoned. At first, no one knew what was wrong with Zelda. They only knew that the huge Bengal tigress's joints were inflamed and swollen, and she could barely walk. Zelda was given medicine to decrease the swelling, as well as antibiotics just in case there was an infection.

Nothing worked. Zelda got even sicker. She could barely move, and her eyes changed to a much darker color. The vet realized that Zelda was bleeding within the eyes. When he took fluid from one of her swollen joints, he found blood in her joints. Zelda was bleeding internally because her blood wasn't clotting. That was when the vet suspected poisoning. The owner of the park was mystified because he knew that no one had poisoned Zelda. How could this have happened?

Rodent populations were controlled by poisoned bait boxes. The poison made it so blood couldn't clot. A rat had eaten the poison, and then it had gone through the fence into Zelda's cage where Zelda had caught and eaten it. What happened to Zelda? She was given shots of vitamin K! Zelda was going to be fine fine.

Check Your Understanding

1. From the context of the passage, you can infer that the vet
   a. didn't know blood needed to clot.
   b. didn't know what rodent poisons could do.
   c. had treated other poisoned animals before.
   d. had never treated a poisoning case before.

2. *Decrease* is to *increase* as
   a. *sick* is to *ill.*
   b. *caught* is to *trapped.*
   c. *mystery* is to *puzzle.*
   d. *internal* is to *external.*

3. From the context of the passage, you can infer that vitamin K
   a. helps blood clot.
   b. helps decrease swelling.
   c. helps bones grow strong.
   d. helps you see better at night.

4. Leafy green vegetables are high in vitamin K. Why wasn't Zelda just given leafy green vegetables?
   a. The dart was too small.
   b. Tigers eat mostly meat.
   c. Zelda wasn't hungry.
   d. Rats had been eating the vegetables.

/4

Warm-Up
18

Name _____

Where Mud Blisters

The Villa Luz cave is located in the southern Mexican state of Tabasco. The cave is deadly. You can't wear a simple oxygen mask. You must wear a mask that provides oxygen, as well as filter out deadly gases. In addition, you must wear special protective clothing. This is because the walls, mud, and water inside the cave are corrosive. One unprotected touch will mean painful red welts and raised blisters.

Despite the dangerous conditions, scientists have gone into the cave. They have scrambled through tight holes. They have waded through chest-deep acidic sulfur springs. They have gone into rooms where the walls dripped acid as strong as battery acid. They have gone to places where, when accidentally scraped against the wall, their radios melted.

Why are the scientists entering such dangerous territory? You would think the cave would be empty of life. Instead, it is teeming with life. The scientists want to study the cave's ecosystem. They want to study the rare food web that is not based on solar power or photosynthesis. What creatures make up the food web and are part of this unique ecosystem? Scientists have found blind fish. They have found bats and poisonous spiders. They have found rooms where the walls are teeming with millions and millions of microbes.

Check Your Understanding

1. Where is the Villa Luz cave located?
a. eastern Mexico
b. western Mexico
c. southern Mexico
d. northern Mexico

2. Another title for the passage might be
a. "A Unique Cave."
b. "All About Microbes."
c. "How Food Webs Work."
d. "The Scientist with the Melted Radio."

3. *Teeming* is to *empty* as
a. *simple* is to *plain*.
b. *painful* is to *hurtful*.
c. *dangerous* is to *unsafe*.
d. *corrosive* is to *healing*.

4. From the context of the passage, what can you infer about food webs?
a. None are based on solar power and photosynthesis.
b. Most are based on solar power and photosynthesis.
c. They are all based on solar power and photosynthesis.
d. Very few are based on solar power and photosynthesis.

/4

Warm-Up 19

Name _____

Squeaking Floors

The Nijo Castle is in Kyoto, Japan. Built in 1603, the castle is famous in part for its floors. What is so special about the castle's floors? Some of the floors squeak! When someone walks on them, even treading lightly, they "chirp" like the nightingale bird.

It is no accident that the floors squeak. They were constructed so they would squeak at the lightest pressure. They were made this way so they could act as a security measure or an alarm system. They kept the royal family safe. Anyone entering the corridors around the royal residence could be heard. It was impossible to enter without making noise. No one could sneak in undetected.

Dry boards will always squeak, but what made these castle floorboards sound like a bird when trod upon? The floors in the corridors surrounding certain rooms were constructed so that the nails for the floorboards passed through a metal clip or clamp. When the slightest pressure was applied, the nails would move against the metal clip. This caused them to "chirp" or sing like a bird. As an added security measure, some of the rooms in the castle also contained special doors. Bodyguards hid behind the doors, ready to come out at a moment's notice.

Check Your Understanding

1. From the context of the passage, you can infer that the squeaking floors were constructed
   a. for every room in the castle.
   b. for every corridor in the castle.
   c. for the bodyguards' special rooms.
   d. for corridors around certain rooms.

2. When something happens and no one knows, it is
   a. safe.
   b. applied.
   c. surrounded.
   d. undetected.

3. Which of the following is *not* true about Nijo Castle?
   a. It is in Korea.
   b. It was built in 1603.
   c. It has floors that "chirp."
   d. It has special doors that you can hide behind.

4. The passage is mainly about
   a. castle defense.
   b. birds in the castle.
   c. who built the castle.
   d. the size of the castle.

/4

Name _____

20   The Salt Is Always on the Table

There is a place where the salt is always on the table. This is because the table is salt! The table does not contain any wood, metal, or plastic materials. The table is constructed entirely of salt. Where is this table? It is in a hotel that, like the table, is constructed entirely of salt. The walls, floors, and even the roof are made out of salt. The tables, chairs, stools, and beds are all carved out of salt.

The largest salt flat, or pan, in the world is in southwestern Bolivia. It is called the Sal de Uyuni. A flat, blindingly white plane, the salt pan is a dried-up lakebed. It covers a surface area of more than 4,000 square miles. Salt is mined from the pan for internal use, as well as for export to other countries. It is estimated that there is more than eleven billion tons of fine salt in the flat.

One clever businessperson decided to make a salt hotel for the tourists who came to view and walk on the salt pan. Salt blocks were cut out of the pan's crust using chainsaws. Then the blocks were fused or cemented together with a paste of salt and water.

Check Your Understanding

1. The largest salt pan in the world is found in
   a. southwestern Bolivia.
   b. southeastern Bolivia.
   c. southwestern Bulgaria.
   d. southeastern Bulgaria.

2. If a product is sent to another country, it is
   a. exported.
   b. imported.
   c. cemented.
   d. estimated.

3. From the context of the passage, you can infer that the salt flat
   a. has a dull surface.
   b. has a soft surface.
   c. has a dark surface.
   d. has a hard surface.

4. The passage is mainly about
   a. a country.
   b. hotels around the world.
   c. a place tourists can stay.
   d. a table that contains plastic.

/4

Warm-Up 21

Name _____

A City Instead of a Plant

Interesting Places and Events

Henri Mahout was a botanist. Mahout was from France. He was in Cambodia in 1860 looking for unknown plant species. While there, he heard about a fabled city. Previously, British explorers had looked for the city, but they hadn't found it. No one was sure if the city really existed. They didn't know if the stories of the city were just fables. Mahout decided to look for the city.

What Mahout found was the ancient city of Angkor. Angkor was the capital city of the Khmer Empire. It was built during the first half of the twelfth century. There were over 1,000 temples in the city. The largest temple is now called Angkor Wat. Angkor Wat is the largest religious building in the world. It is larger than the pyramids. It is larger than the cathedrals in Europe. It is larger than any other temple or church in the world.

Angkor Wat is built facing west. Most temples at that time faced east. The longest day of the year in the Northern Hemisphere is June 21. On that day, the sun rises directly behind the temple's central tower. Imagine going in search of a plant and finding instead such a wondrous city!

Check Your Understanding

1. Which of the following is *not* true about Angkor?
   a. It has over 1,000 temples.
   b. It was built in the twelfth century.
   c. Its largest temple is built facing east.
   d. It was a capital city of the Khmer Empire.

2. The passage is mainly about
   a. Cambodia.
   b. a man from France.
   c. an ancient capital.
   d. the largest building in the world.

3. From the context of the passage, you can infer that botanists study
   a. plants.
   b. cities.
   c. pyramids.
   d. religion.

4. Why might people have thought Angkor was only a fable?
   a. The city never existed.
   b. The city was covered by the jungle.
   c. The city was close to the water.
   d. The city was on a well-traveled path.

 /4

©Teacher Created Resources   29   #5035 Daily Warm-Ups: Nonfiction Reading

Name _____

22 Tunnels in the Netherlands

The Netherlands is a country in Europe. People from the Netherlands speak and are known as Dutch. Much of the Netherlands is flat and below sea level. The Dutch reclaimed the land from the sea. First, they built dikes, or walls, around some land. Then they drained the water from the enclosed area, pumping it into a series of canals so it could drain back into the sea. Now the Dutch are building something else besides dikes. They are building little tunnels that go under their roads and highways. The tunnels are not for draining water or reclaiming land. What purpose could the tunnels have?

Roads are important and necessary. We need them for traveling, as well as for transporting goods. The problem is that roads are often hazardous to wildlife. Badgers are **nocturnal** animals. They live in families in a maze of underground tunnels called "sets." As their natural habitat was destroyed, the badgers needed to forage for food far away from their set.

Unfortunately, many badgers were being hit by cars while on their nightly foraging trips. To keep the badgers safe, the Dutch began to build road fences and special badger tunnels. Infrared cameras and tracks in sand and ink beds show that badgers, as well as foxes, rabbits, and hedgehogs, are using the tunnels.

Check Your Understanding

1. When something is **nocturnal**, it is awake
   a. at night.
   b. during the day.
   c. during the winter.
   d. during the summer.

2. Badgers live in a
   a. den.
   b. set.
   c. nest.
   d. colony.

3. The *Netherlands* is to *Dutch* as
   a. *French* is to *France*.
   b. *German* is to *Germany*.
   c. *Mexico* is to *Spanish*.
   d. *Portuguese* is to *Brazil*.

4. All but what showed that the badgers were using the tunnels under the roads?
   a. infrared cameras
   b. tracks in ink beds
   c. tracks in sand beds
   d. tracks in the dikes

/4

Warm-Up

23

Name _____

A Glowing Meal

A very strange event happened one night. One woman planned an enjoyable evening at home. Her intentions were to watch a movie while eating a delicious dinner of pink shrimp salad. Her plans did not go exactly as she expected. She turned on the movie and switched off the lights. She picked up her salad and started to eat it. That's when she found out that her shrimp salad was glowing!

It so happened that another man left his pink shrimp out to defrost in the sink. Later, when he entered the darkened room, he was shocked to see a glowing mass in his sink. His shrimp were glowing, too! The two events were tied together. They occurred in August 2010. The common factor was the shrimp that had been purchased in stores near the Oregon coast.

The shrimp was not poisoned. It was perfectly safe to eat. What caused the glow-in-the-dark shrimp? Scientists say that the shrimp was covered by luminescent bacteria. The luminescent bacteria may glow, but it is not a health risk. Its presence is not a sign of mishandling during processing. The **luminescent** bacteria grow on sea creatures. It can grow at refrigerator temperatures, especially on seafood products where salt was added during processing.

Check Your Understanding

1. When did this strange event take place?
   a. April 2010
   b. August 2010
   c. October 2010
   d. September 2010

2. According to the passage, if you see a sea creature that glows,
   a. it has to be a shrimp.
   b. it cannot be poisonous.
   c. it has to have been mishandled.
   d. it may be covered with luminescent bacteria.

3. From the context of the passage, you can infer that the shrimp that the man and lady bought
   a. made them ill.
   b. came from different shipments.
   c. had been salted when processed.
   d. was caught in the Gulf of Mexico.

4. When something is **luminescent**, it
   a. glows.
   b. grows.
   c. is safe.
   d. is poisonous.

/4

Name _____

Warm-Up 24

Where Are the Vikings?

There are Norse sagas about the Viking Leif Eriksson. These stories tell of Eriksson sailing from Greenland to Vinland. People said the sagas were fiction. It could not be true. Vinland was not a real place. No one could have settled there around the year 1000.

A map of Vinland was found in 1440. People said the map was a fake. James Cook was an eighteenth-century sea captain from England. Cook figured out that the map of Vinland was a map of what is now northeastern Newfoundland. In 1913, a man named William Munn read the sagas. Using sailing directions, landfall descriptions, and dates, Munn located what he said was Eriksson's landing spot. Some iron nails and Viking boat rivets were found, but that wasn't enough to prove there had been a settlement.

In 1960, a Norwegian man named Helge Ingstad joined the search. Ingstad went to Canada. Then he asked a local Newfoundland fisherman if there were any ruins nearby. Ingstad was sent to what the locals thought were American Indian burial mounds. The mounds were not burial grounds. They were the ruins of Viking sod houses and sod workshops! The ruins were from about the year 1000! You can see the sod buildings today. They have been rebuilt. The site is called L'Anse aux Meadows.

Check Your Understanding

1. Who figured out that the map of Vinland was northeastern Newfoundland?
   a. James Cook
   b. William Munn
   c. Helge Ingstad
   d. Leif Eriksson

2. Which of the following countries is Newfoundland a part of?
   a. Canada
   b. Norway
   c. England
   d. Greenland

3. From the context of the passage, you can infer that
   a. people can change the past.
   b. no one is interested in the past.
   c. people are still learning about the past.
   d. there is nothing new to learn about the past.

4. Which of the following could be a saga?
   a. your birth date
   b. pictures of your school
   c. an old Viking settlement
   d. a long story about a hero

/4

Warm-Up

25

Name _____

A Lake Impossible to Swim In

There is a lake that is impossible to swim in. The water is deep enough, but you wouldn't even want to dip a finger in it. Why wouldn't it be safe to even dip a finger in the lake? The water in the lake is hot and acidic. Your skin would be eaten away!

The beautiful but dangerous lake is called Lake Voui. Lake Voui is on Ambae Island in the South Pacific Ocean. The island is part of the Vanuatu Archipelago. An archipelago is a group of islands. Lake Voui is a crater lake. It is one of two lakes filling the remains of a large volcano that last erupted over four hundred years ago.

Lake Voui is rarely seen from the air, as it is usually capped in rain clouds, but on July 13, 1991, an airline pilot got a good view of it. The pilot was shocked at what he saw. Three areas of the lake were boiling up! Bubbles thirty-three feet in diameter were bursting on its surface. All the vegetation along the edges of the lake had been burned. Every plant was dead. Nothing green remained. The slumbering volcano was waking up!

Check Your Understanding

1. Where is Vanuatu located?
   a. Indian Ocean
   b. Arctic Ocean
   c. Pacific Ocean
   d. Atlantic Ocean

2. Sometimes, boats go out on Lake Voui. Most likely, who is in the boat?
   a. people who are thirsty
   b. people who study volcanoes
   c. people who are catching fish
   d. people who want to go swimming

3. Which of the following U.S. states is an archipelago?
   a. Hawaii
   b. Kansas
   c. Wyoming
   d. New Mexico

4. A synonym for **sleeping** is
   a. burning.
   b. erupting.
   c. bubbling.
   d. slumbering.

/4

Name _____

Warm-Up 26   The State Known for Syrup and Bridges

What state produces the most maple syrup? It is an eastern state. The country of Canada lies to its north. The state of Massachusetts is to the south, New Hampshire is to its east, and New York is to its west. It is one of the smallest states in the Union, and it has one of the smallest populations. Many states have more people living in single cities than living in this entire state! What state is it? It is Vermont, the 14th state to join the Union.

Vermont may be small, but it produces more maple syrup than any other state. Maple syrup does not have any added ingredients. All it contains is boiled sap collected from maple trees. The sap is collected by tapping trees in the spring. When a tree is tapped, a hole is

drilled into it, and a spout is inserted so that its sap can run into a collection bucket.

Over one hundred covered bridges dot Vermont's **rural** landscape. Why were these country bridges from the 1800s covered? The bridges were covered to protect them from extreme weather. People were often charged tolls to cross the bridges. A typical toll for people on foot was one cent, while people on horseback were charged four cents. The fees were used to maintain the bridges.

Check Your Understanding

1. Vermont joined the Union in 1791. How many states belonged to the United States before Vermont joined?
   a. twelve
   b. thirteen
   c. fourteen
   d. fifteen

2. When something is **rural**, it is
   a. covered.
   b. in the city.
   c. charged a toll.
   d. in the country.

3. From the context of the passage, which of the following statements is true?
   a. Canada is on Vermont's eastern border.
   b. New York is on Vermont's northern border.
   c. New Hampshire is on Vermont's western border.
   d. Massachusetts is on Vermont's southern border.

4. Another title for the passage might be
   a. "An Eastern State."
   b. "A Highly Populated State."
   c. "The Biggest State in the Union."
   d. "The Only State with Extreme Weather."

/4

Warm-Up
27

Name _____

Basketball Team Names

The New Orleans Hornets are from New Orleans, Louisiana. Why are they called the Hornets? The name comes from the team's origins, or beginnings. The name's origins go all the way back to the Revolutionary War. Before moving to New Orleans, the team played in North Carolina. The team was called the Charlotte Hornets.

During the Revolutionary War, the British occupied Charlotte. People in the city did not like the British. They made it hard for the British. Lord Cornwallis was a British general. It is said that the general called the city a "nest of hornets." Many years later, people in Charlotte thought this was a good name for their team. After all, hornets will defend themselves fiercely. They will not give up.

The basketball team from Salt Lake City, Utah, is called Utah Jazz. This name goes back to the team's roots. Before moving to Utah, the team played in Louisiana. It was called the New Orleans Jazz. It was called "Jazz" because jazz is a type of music that first **originated** in New Orleans.

The Philadelphia 76ers are from Pennsylvania. The team is commonly referred to as the "Sixers." It is named for the year 1776. This was the year the Declaration of Independence was signed. The declaration was signed in Philadelphia.

Check Your Understanding

1. What city correctly goes with what state?
   a. New Orleans, Utah
   b. Pennsylvania, Louisiana
   c. Charlotte, North Carolina
   d. Salt Lake City, Pennsylvania

2. Which of the following is a synonym for **originated**?
   a. named
   b. occupied
   c. defended
   d. began

3. From the context of the passage, you can infer that
   a. a team's name can never change.
   b. a team's name may change over time.
   c. a city has to be part of a team's name.
   d. a state has to be part of a team's name.

4. If someone says you are like a hornet, he or she might mean that you are
   a. weak.
   b. sleepy.
   c. fierce.
   d. unhappy.

/4

Warm-Up

28

Name _____

Grasshoppers in Ice

Some grasshoppers were sent to a lab in 1914. The people in the lab said that the grasshoppers were really migratory locusts. They crossed the country in great swarms. They would eat everything in their path. The interesting thing about these locusts is that they were thought to be extinct. They've been dead for over two hundred years. Where had these locusts come from?

The locusts were found in the Beartooth Mountain Range. These rough, rugged mountains are in Montana. Montana is a western state. It is bordered by Canada to the north, Idaho to the west, Wyoming to the south, and North Dakota to the east. The locusts were found in a glacier. Years ago, a swarm of locusts must have been passing over the high mountain range. Somehow, they became chilled and dropped onto the ice. They became covered with snow and ice. Soon, they became buried in the glacier.

The glacier was given the name Grasshopper Glacier. Many intact locusts have been removed from the glacier. Today, the glacier is disappearing because, with warmer temperatures, the ice is melting. As the ice has melted, many more locusts have been exposed. As the locusts have defrosted, they have begun to rot. The melting ice is causing the found locusts to become extinct once more!

Check Your Understanding

1. Which of the following answers is true?
   a. Idaho is to the north of Montana.
   b. Canada is to the south of Montana.
   c. Wyoming is to the west of Montana.
   d. North Dakota is to the east of Montana.

2. What might have caused the locusts to be on the glacier?
   a. They flew down to eat.
   b. They were caught in a sudden storm.
   c. They wanted to stop flying in a swarm.
   d. They landed to cool down when temperatures rose.

3. Which adjective does *not* describe the Beartooth Mountain Range?
   a. high
   b. rough
   c. intact
   d. rugged

4. The passage is mainly about
   a. extinct locusts in Montana.
   b. what swarms of locusts ate.
   c. warming temperatures and disappearing glaciers.
   d. the difference between grasshoppers and locusts.

/4

Warm-Up

29

Name _____

Hadrian's Wall

There is a wall in England that many people go to see. Some people even take a special walking trail that goes alongside the wall. What makes this wall so special? Who would build such a wall? Why would anyone be interested in seeing or walking alongside it?

The wall is called Hadrian's Wall. The wall extends across the entire width of northern England. It is about 73 miles long. When constructed, the wall was made from stones and turf. Turf, or sod, is a top layer of earth containing grass with its roots. The stone parts were about 10 feet wide and 16–20 feet high. The turf parts were about 20 feet wide and 11.5 feet high. Parts of the wall have collapsed, but large sections still snake across the land.

People who walk alongside this wall enjoy the moorland landscape, but they also are looking at history. This is because the wall was the most heavily fortified border in the Roman Empire! The Roman emperor Hadrian ordered the wall built in 122 CE. It was completed in just eight years and marked the northern border of Roman territory. Gates, watchtowers, and forts were built into and along the wall.

Check Your Understanding

1. The passage is mainly about
  a. a walking path.
  b. an old Roman wall.
  c. the Roman emperor Hadrian.
  d. the boundaries of the Roman Empire.

2. How long did it take for the wall to be built?
  a. eight years
  b. eighteen years
  c. eighty years
  d. eighty-eight years

3. From the context of the passage, you can infer
  a. when the Roman Empire collapsed.
  b. when the British Empire collapsed.
  c. that a country never changes its borders.
  d. that a country's borders may change over time.

4. When something is "made stronger," it is
  a. completed.
  b. collapsed.
  c. fortified.
  d. constructed.

/4

Warm-Up
30

Name _____

Sleeping in a Capsule

When most people think of a hotel room, they think of a room they can comfortably walk around in. They think of a room furnished with a bed, nightstand, dresser, chair, and desk. They know the room will have its own bathroom. If this is what they expect, they might be very surprised when they go to some hotels in Japan.

Capsule hotels are quite different. Capsule hotels do not provide rooms. Instead, they provide tiny capsules for sleeping. The capsules are stacked side by side and on top of each other without any space in between. Each capsule measures about three by four by six feet. You can't stand up, but you can stretch out.

The capsules have only one open end, but there is a curtain you can pull across the opening for privacy. Each capsule has a small television, light, and alarm clock. The guests share bathrooms. They are also given a key to a locker that can hold a small bag.

You might **scoff** at such accommodations, but they cost much less than larger hotel rooms. They are perfect for business people who can't get home for the night or for travelers set on spending their money on seeing sights and dining rather than sleeping accommodations.

Check Your Understanding

1. According to the passage, capsule hotels are in
   a. Japan.
   b. Jamaica.
   c. Algeria.
   d. Argentina.

2. You might find capsule hotels in crowded cities because
   a. there are fewer sights to see there.
   b. people eat more in crowded cities.
   c. more people can fit in less space.
   d. city people don't carry large bags.

3. What kind of person would be least likely to stay in a capsule hotel?
   a. one who likes to travel lightly
   b. one who is trying to save money
   c. one who doesn't want a fancy room
   d. one who doesn't like feeling closed in

4. When you **scoff** at something, you
   a. make fun of it.
   b. spend money on it.
   c. stretch out in it.
   d. praise and admire it.

/4

Scientifically Speaking

Warm-Up 1

Name _____

A Weighty Puzzle

There are two siblings. They are identical twin brothers. Everything about them is exactly the same. Their clothes and shoes are identical. Their hairstyles and hair lengths are identical. They eat the same type and quantity of food. They are identical, but they are different weights. How can this be possible?

The answer lies in where the siblings are located. One twin is at the North Pole, while one twin is at the equator. Earth is not a perfect sphere. It bulges slightly at the equator. When something bulges, it pushes out. This means that the twin at the North Pole is closer to the center of Earth. The twin at the equator is slightly further away from the center of Earth.

The brothers' locations affect the pull of gravity on their bodies. The closer you are to Earth's core, the greater the gravitational force. The farther away you are from Earth's core, the lighter the gravitational force. The lighter the gravitational force, the less you weigh. Suppose the twin at the North Pole weighs 100 pounds. At the equator, his identical sibling would weigh slightly less. He would only weigh 99.5 pounds.

Check Your Understanding

1. A sibling
   a. cannot be a twin.
   b. is never identical.
   c. can only be a sister.
   d. is a sister or a brother.

2. Suppose you weigh 100 pounds. On the moon, you would weigh 16.6 pounds. This is because the moon's gravitational force
   a. is lighter than Earth's.
   b. is greater than Earth's.
   c. is the same as Earth's.
   d. is identical to Earth's.

3. At what location would you most likely weigh the least?
   a. the top of a ladder
   b. the top of a skyscraper
   c. the top of Mount Everest
   d. the top of a redwood tree

4. *Box* is to *square* as
   a. *sphere* is to *core*.
   b. *sphere* is to *round*.
   c. *sphere* is to *bulge*.
   d. *sphere* is to *equator*.

/4

Name _____

A Living Dragon

Komodo dragons live in Indonesia. They are the largest lizards in the world. Males can grow up to ten feet long and weigh up to 176 pounds. These huge reptiles are carnivores. Carnivores eat only meat. A Komodo dragon can eat 80 percent of its body weight in just one meal. This means that if a dragon weighed 100 pounds, it could eat 80 pounds of meat at one time!

Using their long, yellow tongues, Komodo dragons can smell prey one mile away. A Komodo dragon will hide, and when its unsuspecting prey passes by, it attacks. Often, the Komodo dragon will merely bite its prey and then let it go. This way the lizard is safe from battle injuries, but it is also guaranteed a meal.

Why is the lizard's meal guaranteed? The Komodo dragon has sixty serrated, or notched, teeth. The dragon uses its serrated teeth to rip into its prey's flesh. Then, using special venom glands in its mouth, the lizard injects poison into the wound. Once the venom is injected, the dragon lets its prey go. A fight is no longer needed. All the lizard has to do is follow its victim and wait for its prey to die from loss of blood and poison.

Check Your Understanding

1. Where are a Komodo dragon's venom glands?
   a. in its claws
   b. in its mouth
   c. in its teeth
   d. in its tongue

2. The passage is
   a. fiction.
   b. full of facts.
   c. full of opinions.
   d. about the future.

3. Which of the following objects is serrated?
   a. the blade of a saw
   b. the edge of a ruler
   c. the handle of a hammer
   d. the tip of a screwdriver

4. Another title for the passage might be
   a. "The Smallest Meal."
   b. "The Animals of Indonesia."
   c. "The Life of the Komodo Dragon."
   d. "The Largest Lizard and Its Food."

/4

Name _____

Pop Goes the Knuckle

You may have seen (or heard) people who bend their fingers back or pull on their joints. You hear a loud *CRACK!* What exactly is that **audible** popping sound? Are they really cracking their knuckles? Believe it or not, they did not crack anything. What they did do is burst bubbles.

Your knuckles are joints. Joints are where two separate bones meet and are held together by connective tissues and ligaments. Every joint in your body is surrounded by a sac of synovial fluid. Synovial fluid is a thick, clear liquid.

When you stretch or pull on your joints, you also stretch the sac of synovial fluid. When you stretch the sac, you are making more space inside of it. You are increasing

its volume. This reduces the pressure inside it. When the pressure is decreased, gases that were dissolved in the fluid form bubbles. If the sac is stretched further, the volume increases even more, and the pressure becomes even less. When the pressure is low enough, the bubbles will burst. They will crack open with a loud, audible pop.

After cracking the knuckles once, can they be cracked again immediately after? No, they can't, at least for about thirty minutes! This is because it takes time for the gas to dissolve back into the synovial fluid.

Check Your Understanding

1. When something is **audible**, it can be
   a. heard.
   b. opened.
   c. stretched.
   d. dissolved.

2. Which of the following is *not* true about your knuckles?
   a. They are joints.
   b. They are where two bones meet.
   c. They are made of a clear, thick fluid.
   d. They are held together by connective tissues.

3. *Before* is to *after* as
   a. *stretch* is to *pull*.
   b. *dissolve* is to *melt*.
   c. *immediately* is to *now*.
   d. *increase* is to *decrease*.

4. From the context of the passage, which of the following causes the bubbles?
   a. gas
   b. joints
   c. ligaments
   d. synovial fluid

/4

Warm-Up

Name _____

4   Lightning Strikes Twice

Some people say that lightning never strikes the same place twice. These people are wrong. Lightning is more likely to strike a place it has struck before. Why is this so? Lightning is an atmospheric discharge of electricity. Lightning storms are common. Worldwide, there are about sixteen million storms every year.

When lightning strikes, it usually hits the highest point within a radius of about one hundred feet. This means that a tall tree in an open field may be hit over and over. The Empire State Building, in New York City, is struck about one hundred times a year. Believe it or not, this is on purpose. A huge twenty-two-story antenna was attached to the top of the building in 1985. The antenna acts as a lightning rod to protect **surrounding** buildings.

Will you be struck by lightning? It is not very likely. There are some people who have been struck by lightning though. For example, Roy Sullivan, who was a park ranger in Virginia, survived seven lightning strikes. His first strike was when he was in a fire lookout tower. The tower was new, and it didn't have a lightning rod yet. The lightning burned a strip of Sullivan's right leg and left a hole in his shoe.

Check Your Understanding

1. If the passage was longer, it might talk about
    a. other times Sullivan was struck.
    b. how tall fire lookout towers are.
    c. Sullivan's trip to New York City.
    d. why Sullivan became a park ranger.

2. A tree gets hit. A taller tree does not get hit. Most likely, the taller tree
    a. was over 10 feet away.
    b. was over 100 feet away at least.
    c. was over 1,000 feet away at least.
    d. was over 10,000 feet away at least.

3. From the context of the passage, you can infer that
    a. you cannot protect yourself from lightning.
    b. you cannot survive being struck by lightning.
    c. there are very few lightning storms worldwide.
    d. there are ways to protect yourself from lightning.

4. When you **surround** something, you
    a. go into its center.
    b. burn a hole through it.
    c. enclose or go around it.
    d. make an atmospheric discharge.

/4

Name _____

Danger! Exploding Seeds!

The sandbox tree has a unique way to spread its seeds. It launches them, shooting them out like powerful missiles. When the seed capsule explodes, it sounds like a loud firecracker. The round, flattened seeds are about 3/4 of an inch in diameter. The seeds explode with such force that they can shoot over three hundred feet! They can even harm humans and livestock!

This type of seed spreading is called mechanical dispersal. There are other plants that disperse, or spread, their seeds in the same way, but no other plant does it with such force.

The sandbox tree is an evergreen tree that can reach heights of over 120 feet. It is native to tropical regions in North and South America. It has smooth brown bark that is covered in many dark, pointed spines. In some areas, the tree is known as the monkey no-climb tree because of these spines. Its leaves are papery thin, heart-shaped, and up to two feet long. The tree has **caustic**, milky sap that is poisonous. (When something is *caustic*, it burns.) Long ago, people called the Caribs dipped the tips of their arrows in the poisonous sap. The wood of the sandbox tree is yellow or brown and is used for furniture.

Check Your Understanding

1. Why is the Sandbox tree known to some as the monkey no-climb tree?
   a. It has caustic sap.
   b. It has smooth bark.
   c. It is covered in spines.
   d. It has explosive seed capsules.

2. What two parts of the tree could cause harm to humans and animals?
   a. bark and sap
   b. seeds and sap
   c. sap and leaves
   d. spines and leaves

3. What is the opposite of **caustic**?
   a. burning
   b. pinching
   c. stinging
   d. soothing

4. If a plant spreads its seeds by mechanical dispersal,
   a. its seed capsule breaks open.
   b. its seed capsule floats on the wind.
   c. its seed capsule must be papery thin.
   d. its seed capsule is carried by animals.

/4

Warm-Up 6   Name _____

Lethal to Nonlethal

A person gets bitten by a Sydney funnel web spider in 1980. The bite is **lethal**. The person dies. A person gets bitten by a Sydney funnel web spider in 1982. The bite isn't lethal. The person lives. What happened in 1981?

The Sydney funnel web spider is one of the most dangerous spiders in the world. It lives in Australia. People are usually bitten by males. This is because males wander around looking for females. The male may end up in a shoe or a piece of clothing left on the floor. It may end up in a swimming pool where it can survive for several hours. The spiders are aggressive. They use their fangs to inject venom, or poison, into their victims.

Before 1981, there was no way to treat a victim. In 1981, an antivenom was made. How is an antivenom made? First, a small amount of venom is injected into an animal. This makes the animal produce antibodies. Antibodies are proteins. They float in the blood. They identify and attack foreign objects. The antibodies make the animal immune to the poison. It is these antibodies that are used to make antivenom. The antibodies in the antivenom will identify the poison in the victim's body. They will then attack and disable it.

Check Your Understanding

1. Which of the following is *not* true about Sydney funnel web spiders?
a. They are aggressive.
b. They are poisonous.
c. They live in Australia.
d. Females look for males.

2. When something is **lethal**, it is
a. immune.
b. deadly.
c. injected.
d. disabled.

3. What was needed to make the antivenom for the Sydney funnel web spider?
a. venom from the spider
b. fangs from the male spider
c. antibodies from the spider
d. a spider's victim before 1981

4. Most likely, what might an emergency room have in it?
a. antivenom for most poisonous animals
b. antibodies for most poisonous animals
c. antivenom for local poisonous animals
d. antibodies for local poisonous animals

/4

Name _____

An Animal Like a Raincoat

The Brazilian pygmy gecko is a tiny lizard. It is so small that it can sit comfortably on your fingertip. It is so light that, if a pygmy gecko is sitting on a leaf and a raindrop lands on the leaf, the pygmy gecko is bounced up into the air! It is so small that it could be battered by a raindrop landing on it. It is so small that it could easily drown in a tiny puddle.

Yet the pygmy gecko has something unique. It has something that helps it to survive in the rainforest where it lives and where it rains all the time. What unique thing does the lightest lizard in the world have that is essential to its survival? It has its skin.

The lizard's skin is hydrophobic. That means its skin is like a raincoat. It is waterproof. It repels water. It keeps the gecko from getting wet in all the rain. In addition, the pygmy gecko can run across water without sinking. This is because it is so light that it does not break the water surface tension. Instead, it floats on the water's surface. The combination of its lightness and its hydrophobic skin makes the pygmy gecko nearly unsinkable.

Check Your Understanding

1. A tiny, shallow puddle to us might seem like
   a. a fingertip to the pygmy gecko.
   b. a large, deep lake to the pygmy gecko.
   c. a battering raindrop to the pygmy gecko.
   d. a waterproof raincoat to the pygmy gecko.

2. A leaf may float on water because
   a. leaves cannot get wet.
   b. the water is hydrophobic.
   c. the leaf has been battered by rain.
   d. the water surface tension is unbroken.

3. From the context of the passage, which of the following statements is true?
   a. No geckos are lizards.
   b. No lizards are geckos.
   c. All lizards are geckos.
   d. none of the above

4. *Attract* is to *repel* as
   a. *float* is to *sink*.
   b. *survive* is to *live*.
   c. *essential* is to *necessary*.
   d. *combination* is to *mixture*.

/4

Warm-Up
8

Name _____

One Plant, Two Cats

Two cats see a plant. One cat seems to go crazy. For several minutes, it wildly rubs itself against the plant, rolls over it, and even kicks at it. Then the cat suddenly loses interest and walks away. The other cat has no reaction at all. Two hours later, the same thing occurs. The cat that went wild over the plant goes wild again, and the cat that ignored it pays no attention. What is the plant, and why is one cat affected while the other is not?

The plant, called "catnip," is a perennial herb of the mint family. (A perennial plant, unlike an annual plant, does not have to be replanted every year.) Catnip contains **pungent** oil that cats can smell. The strong-smelling oil contains a chemical called trans-neptalactone.

This chemical closely resembles a pungent excretion found in female cat urine.

The reaction to catnip is an inherited trait. If a cat's parents are affected by catnip, then its offspring will likely be affected, too. Very young kittens and older cats usually don't have a reaction. If a cat does have a reaction, it acclimates after a short time. Then it takes about an hour or two for the cat to "reset," and once again, the cat will go crazy over a plant.

Check Your Understanding

1. Which of the following answers is *not* a perennial plant?
  a. sunflower
  b. rose bush
  c. pine tree
  d. apple tree

2. A cat goes wild over catnip. From the context of the passage, one can infer that the cat
  a. is very old.
  b. is a young kitten.
  c. has parents that reacted to catnip.
  d. has parents that didn't react to catnip.

3. If a smell is **pungent**, it is
  a. a soft or fresh odor.
  b. a light or breezy odor.
  c. a sweet or flowery odor.
  d. a sharp or stinging odor.

4. The passage is mainly about
  a. cats that go wild.
  b. cats and a kind of herb.
  c. chemicals cats can smell.
  d. different traits cats can inherit.

/4

Warm-Up
9

Name _____

What Could Be Humming?

The woods are filled with snow, and the temperature is below freezing. Despite the snow and freezing temperature, there is a loud, continuous humming. What in the world could be making that sound? Believe it or not, it is the sound of newborn brown bear cubs! While nursing, newborn brown bear cubs produce a loud, continuous humming that is loud enough to be heard from outside of the bear's den! The humming stimulates their mother's milk production.

Brown bears spend four to six months a year in a deep sleep. While bears are in this winter sleep, their metabolism slows down, and their heartbeat goes from seventy beats a minute to ten. They do not urinate or defecate all winter. The mother bear doesn't wake up, even when she gives birth!

There are usually two cubs, and they are born hairless, toothless, and with eyes sealed shut. They spend the winter feeding and keeping warm in their mother's fur. As they get bigger, their eyes open, and they grow teeth and fur. They play and wrestle with each other, safe inside the den. When their mother wakes up, they are ready to follow her outside. They will have grown all winter, while their mother will have gotten smaller. She will have lost about one-third of her body weight.

Check Your Understanding

1. The mother bear will have lost so much weight, in part, because
   a. her metabolism slowed down.
   b. she did not urinate or defecate.
   c. she was feeding milk to her cubs.
   d. her heartbeat went from seventy to ten.

2. Brown bears in zoos spend much less time in winter sleep. This may be because
   a. they are fed and their cages are warm.
   b. the mother will have grown all winter.
   c. their cubs are born with teeth and fur.
   d. they usually only give birth to one cub.

3. A brown bear's heartbeat may go down by how many beats?
   a. fifty
   b. sixty
   c. seventy
   d. eighty

4. If something gets you active or gets you going, it is
   a. humming.
   b. nursing.
   c. continuous.
   d. stimulating.

/4

Warm-Up
10

Name _____

Into a Hurricane

Hurricane Hugo struck in September 1989. Scientists flew into the eye of the hurricane. They wanted to collect data so they could better understand how hurricanes form and behave. The scientists were stationed in Florida, but for this trip they left from the island of Barbados. A journalist from Barbados flew with the scientists.

The scientists were used to turbulence. They expected it. However, this time the turbulence was worse than usual. The scientists weren't sure they were going to survive. A twenty-man life raft that had been strapped to the deck broke loose. It flew to the ceiling and dented a metal handrail. The galley was trashed, and soda cans, coffee, peanut butter, and paperwork flew through the air. The

toilet overflowed, spewing waste all over the floor. To make matters worse, a thirty-foot long flame was shooting from the back of one of the engines, and they had to shut it down. There was a high risk that they were going to crash into the ocean.

With only thirty seconds to spare, the plane was able to gain altitude. The scientists and pilots were greatly relieved. The journalist had remained quiet during all the excitement. It ended up that she thought what had happened was normal! The scientists had to tell her how bad it had been.

Check Your Understanding

1. From the context of the passage, you can infer that the scientists
   a. had flown into hurricanes before.
   b. thought hurricanes were all the same.
   c. didn't want a journalist on board.
   d. were not expecting any turbulence.

2. Most likely, if the journalist had previously flown into other hurricanes, she would have been more
   a. calm.
   b. happy.
   c. scared.
   d. relaxed.

3. When something "spews out," it
   a. stays in.
   b. drips out.
   c. gushes out.
   d. trickles out.

4. When a plane gains altitude,
   a. it goes higher.
   b. it stops shaking.
   c. it gets closer to land.
   d. it gets closer to water.

/4

Name _____

Warm-Up

11

Positive Identification

You can be identified by your fingerprints. This is because your fingerprints are unique. No one else has the exact same lines and swirls. Now there is another part of your body that can be used for identification. What body part can be used for positive identification? It is none other than your eye.

The colored part of your eye is called the iris. The iris is a circular muscle. It controls the size of the pupil so that more or less light is allowed to enter the eye. The pattern of marks in the iris is as unique as a fingerprint. Every iris has its own unique pattern. This means that each of your eyes has its own pattern. Even identical twins have different iris patterns. The pattern does not change as

you get older. It stays the same all throughout your life.

With iris recognition, a small camera takes an instant photograph of your eye. The photograph is translated into a digital form called a *biometric code*. No one will have the same biometric code because no one has the same pattern of marks. The advantage of iris recognition is that it is fast, and you don't have to touch anything. In addition, people wearing contact lenses or glasses can still be identified.

Check Your Understanding

1. How does iris recognition work?
   a. Marks in the pupil are put into a digital form.
   b. Marks in the iris are put into a biometric code.
   c. A photograph is taken of a person's fingerprint.
   d. The amount of light entering the pupil is put into code.

2. *Unique* is to *common* as
   a. *enter* is to *exit*.
   b. *change* is to *alter*.
   c. *allow* is to *permit*.
   d. *identify* is to *name*.

3. In total, how many different iris patterns are there with identical twins?
   a. one
   b. two
   c. three
   d. four

4. If someone is *not* recognized using iris recognition, it might be because
   a. they were wearing glasses.
   b. they were wearing contact lenses.
   c. they blinked when the picture was taken.
   d. a long time had passed between photographs.

/4

Warm-Up

12

Name _____

The Amazing Cat

There is a cat that is incredibly strong. This cat can climb fifty feet up in a tree while holding a dead animal that is larger and heavier than itself in its mouth! This cat can leap twenty feet in a single bound. It can jump ten feet straight up. This cat can reach speeds up to thirty-six miles an hour. If you think you can escape this cat by getting into the water, you are mistaken. This cat not only likes water, but it is a very strong swimmer. Exactly what kind of cat is this amazing animal?

The cat is a leopard. Leopards are known for their flower-shaped spots called *rosettes*. Usually a leopard's rosettes do not have a central spot. Rosettes help camouflage the leopard, helping it to stay hidden in shifting shadows and shade. Even though you may have trouble seeing spots on a dark leopard (commonly called black panthers), the rosettes are present.

Leopards drag their prey high into trees to protect it. They want to keep it safe from other predators, such as lions or hyenas. Rather than their sense of smell, leopards use their keen sense of sight and hearing to find their prey. A leopard's hearing is so developed that it can hear five times more sounds than humans.

Check Your Understanding

1. From the context of the passage, you can infer that
   a. leopards only live near streams.
   b. leopards are all the same color.
   c. there are sounds humans can't hear.
   d. leopards cannot smell as well as humans.

2. From the context of the passage, which of the following statements is correct?
   a. Leopards can jump twenty feet straight up.
   b. Leopards can climb thirty-six miles up in a tree.
   c. Leopards can leap thirty-six feet in a single bound.
   d. Leopards can carry larger and heavier animals than themselves.

3. If you see a large, black cat,
   a. it may be a leopard.
   b. it cannot be a leopard.
   c. it cannot have rosettes.
   d. it will not like the water.

4. The passage is mainly about
   a. all kinds of cats.
   b. one kind of predator.
   c. senses used for hunting.
   d. what camouflages leopards.

/4

Warm-Up

13   Invasion of Wings

Name _____

What is one of the most common and abundant birds in the United States? It is the starling. Starlings are stocky black birds. They have short tails and triangular wings. They are dark and glossy in the summer, and in the winter, they are covered with white spots. Starlings are loud and aggressive. They travel in large flocks.

Starlings are not native to North America. They are an invasive species. Once introduced, they quickly adapted. They spread across the United States. Their success came at a cost. Native bird species could not compete with the aggressive starlings for nesting holes. As a result, the numbers of native birds greatly declined.

Was this invasive and destructive species brought here by accident? No, it was done on purpose! A man named Eugene Schieffelin released a flock of sixty starlings in New York's Central Park in 1890. He released another flock of forty birds in 1891. Why did Schieffelin release the birds? It is said that he wanted to introduce all the birds mentioned in Shakespeare's works. (Shakespeare was a famous English poet and playwright.) Today, it is estimated that there are more than 200 million starlings in the United States. It makes you wonder what Schieffelin would think if he were alive today.

Check Your Understanding

1. If Schieffelin had *not* released starlings, the native bird population of the United States
   a. would have declined.
   b. would be 200 million.
   c. might be quite different today.
   d. would be exactly the same as it is today.

2. From the context of the passage, you can infer that starlings spread across the United States from
   a. east to west.
   b. west to east.
   c. south to east.
   d. south to north.

3. *Starling* is to *flock* as
   a. *cat* is to *meow*.
   b. *wolf* is to *pack*.
   c. *dog* is to *puppy*.
   d. *horse* is to *ride*.

4. What kind of person is overly aggressive?
   a. one who can adapt
   b. one who wants to do well
   c. one who tries to get along
   d. one who is ready to start fights

/4

Name _____

Strolling Across Venus

Suppose that you could get to Venus, the second planet from the sun. Suppose you tried to stroll across its surface. It would not feel the same as walking across Earth. It would feel like you were walking across a swimming pool underwater. Why would it feel this way?

Each planet has a different makeup of air with different amounts of gases. Earth's air is made up of nitrogen (about 77 percent), oxygen (about 21 percent), and other gases. Though it may not seem like it, air has weight. Scientists weigh air by measuring how much it presses against objects on Earth. On Earth, there is on average 14.7 pounds of pressure per square inch. (The pressure gets less the higher you go, as the air gets thinner.)

The air on Venus is a thick layer of carbon dioxide gas. It would press down on you with more than 1,300 pounds of force instead of 14.7! All the weight and pressure would make you feel like you were walking underwater.

Contrast this to strolling on Mars. The air on Mars is mainly carbon dioxide, and it is very thin. It would only press down on you with about one pound of force per square inch.

Check Your Understanding

1. From the context of the passage, you can infer that
   a. Earth's air would feel lighter than Mars'.
   b. Mars' air would feel lighter than Earth's.
   c. Venus's air would feel lighter than Mars'.
   d. Venus's air would feel lighter than Earth's.

2. In the passage, what were you told about Venus but *not* Earth or Mars?
   a. the makeup of its air
   b. when it was discovered
   c. its average air pressure
   d. its position from the sun

3. *Stroll* is to *walk* as
   a. *jump* is to *leap*.
   b. *swim* is to *water*.
   c. *hop* is to *rabbit*.
   d. *breathe* is to *air*.

4. From the context of the passage, you can infer that if you dropped a penny on Venus, it would
   a. fall to the ground like on Earth.
   b. float up into the air like a balloon.
   c. slowly flutter down as if falling through water.
   d. smash down to the ground as if it were a heavy rock.

/4

Name _____

All About the Jump

Most mammals can jump. The impala, an African antelope, is an exceptional jumper. The impala can jump almost twelve feet in the air. With a running start, the impala can spring forward thirty feet.

There are other mammals, on the other hand, that can barely jump or can't jump at all. Among the animals that can't jump are elephants and rhinoceroses. This is not surprising when you think about how extremely heavy these two animals are. It would take a tremendous burst of energy to lift these massive beasts off the ground.

The pronghorn is a native American species. Many people call it an antelope, but the pronghorn is in its own family. The pronghorn is the fastest mammal in the New World. It has been clocked at speeds of up to fifty-three miles per hour. Most people assume that the pronghorn is an excellent jumper. The truth is that the pronghorn is a horrible jumper. If the pronghorn comes to a fence, it will not jump over it. Instead, it will try to crawl under it! This inability to jump well has hurt the pronghorn. This is because ranchers have built fences. The fences prevent the pronghorn from migrating. It stops them from finding mates. Sometimes, it leads to them being unable to find enough food.

Check Your Understanding

1. What animals are mentioned in the passage?
   a. elephant, rhinoceros, monkey
   b. rhinoceros, pronghorn, impala
   c. antelope, rhinoceros, buffalo
   d. impala, hippopotamus, pronghorn

2. Why can't the elephant jump?
   a. It is too heavy.
   b. It doesn't have knees.
   c. It is not an antelope.
   d. It is an Old World species.

3. Most likely, what happened to pronghorns when ranchers first settled on the prairies?
   a. The population went up.
   b. The population died out.
   c. The population went down.
   d. The population stayed the same.

4. When a scientist refers to a New World species, the scientist is talking about an animal that
   a. is from Africa.
   b. is a good jumper.
   c. is newly discovered.
   d. is from the Americas.

/4

Name _____

What Cut Time?

In 1952, a plane flew from Tokyo to Honolulu in one-third the time it usually took. Not only did the plane fly faster, but it also used less fuel. How did the plane fly faster and use less fuel? How did the pilot cut the time?

The pilot used the jet stream! We use the singular "jet stream," but there are several jet streams. Jet streams are like narrow, rushing currents of air. They are found only at high altitudes. The currents were called "jet stream" because a jet is a forceful flow of liquid or gas from a nozzle or spout. There are two main jet streams in each hemisphere. The main jet streams usually blow west to east over the warm subtropics and cold polar regions. Sometimes, the two jet streams merge into one, and other times there is a third jet stream.

Most people learned about the jet streams during World War II. Pilots returned to the ground with tales of almost coming to a standstill as they tried to fly against these ferocious ribbons of wind. The jet stream usually blows at speeds ranging from 60 to 150 miles per hour, but there are times when they blow 310 miles per hour.

Check Your Understanding

1. A jet stream is most like an
   a. ocean tide.
   b. ocean wave.
   c. ocean storm.
   d. ocean current.

2. A plane flying from coast to coast may go faster in one direction than the other
   a. if it flies at night.
   b. if it flies with the jet stream.
   c. if it goes against the jet stream.
   d. if it stays out of the jet stream.

3. Most likely, we began to learn more about the jet stream when
   a. people had invented better telescopes.
   b. scientists did experiments with kites.
   c. planes began to fly at higher altitudes.
   d. scientists began to study planes.

4. Jet streams most usually blow
   a. west to east.
   b. east to west.
   c. north to south.
   d. south to north.

/4

Name _____

Bee Air Conditioning

Honeybees live in hives. On hot, sweltering days, how do honeybees regulate the hive temperature? How do they keep the hive cool? The bees make their own air conditioning. They reduce the temperature within the hive by circulating the air.

Bees use their wings as fans. The number of fanning bees depends on the hive conditions. Sometimes, just a few bees fan. Other times, it may be several hundred. The fanning bees stand at one side of the hive entrance. They stand just far enough apart so that they don't interfere with each other's movement. They all face the same direction, so as to draw air out of the hive. Then they fan their wings with such vigor that they set up out-going air currents at that half of the entrance. At times,

half of the bottom board of the hive, from front to back, may be covered with fanning bees.

In extreme conditions, another group of fanning bees will take up position on the other entrance half. They will face the opposite direction, thus increasing the flow of air passing into the hive. Air circulation within the hive is greatly increased, as air at one end of the entrance is being drawn in, while at the other end of the entrance, it is being drawn out.

Check Your Understanding

1. Which of the following is *not* true about the fanning bees?
   a. They fan on the bottom board.
   b. They stand close enough to touch.
   c. They fan at one end of the entrance.
   d. They stand at one entrance side and face the same direction.

2. *In* is to *out* as
   a. *sweltering* is to *hot*.
   b. *sweltering* is to *vigor*.
   c. *sweltering* is to *freezing*.
   d. *sweltering* is to *regulate*.

3. It is extremely hot. Most likely, how many bees are fanning?
   a. 3
   b. 30
   c. 130
   d. 300

4. When would you feel air circulating?
   a. when you wave a fan
   b. when you eat ice cream
   c. when you sip a cold drink
   d. when you dive into a swimming pool

/4

Name _____

Yucky Breath

Morning breath can be really yucky. You brush your teeth before going to bed. You don't eat anything during the night. Why is your breath so **foul** in the morning?

Bad breath is caused by bacteria in our mouths. The bacteria live off of tiny particles of food. The waste products of the bacteria emit stinky sulfur gases. These bacteria are anaerobic. Anaerobic bacteria like to live where there is little or no oxygen.

Saliva is a clear liquid that is made in our mouth. We produce about two to four pints of saliva every day. We need all this saliva because it wets food and makes it easier to swallow. It allows us to taste, as a dry tongue can't tell how things taste. Saliva also helps start the process of digestion.

Saliva is made up of mostly water. Water is made up of hydrogen and oxygen. Our saliva ends up acting like an antibacterial mouthwash because of all the oxygen it contains. At night, our saliva production goes down. We don't need as much because we're not eating. As our mouth dries out, the bacteria multiply. More bacteria mean more waste products. More waste products lead to stinky, foul breath.

Check Your Understanding

1. Why does our saliva act like an antibacterial mouthwash?
- a. It has oxygen in it.
- b. It allows us to taste.
- c. It is produced in our mouth.
- d. It starts the process of digestion.

2. What type of bacteria doesn't need oxygen to survive?
- a. spiral
- b. aerobic
- c. sulfuric
- d. anaerobic

3. All but what is a synonym for **foul**?
- a. dirty
- b. clean
- c. stinky
- d. polluted

4. Who might have the sweetest breath in the morning?
- a. a person who sleeps in
- b. a person with a dry mouth
- c. a person who works at night
- d. a person who doesn't brush his or her teeth

/4

Name _____

The Strongest

A wolverine belongs to the weasel family. It is the largest and fiercest member. It is no bigger than a medium-sized dog, but its strength is legendary. Despite its size, it can take down moose or reindeer. Sometimes, it chases much larger animals away from their own kills. It will even take away prey from grizzly bears or mountain lions! It is said that if a wolverine were as large as a bear, it would be the strongest animal on Earth.

Wolverines are native to the northern regions of North America, Europe, and Asia. It is very cold in these areas. Food can be scarce. Some animals survive by migrating. Others hibernate. Wolverines do not migrate or hibernate. They continue to hunt and scavenge for food all winter.

Wolverines can smell food even underneath the snow. It doesn't matter if the food is frozen solid. A wolverine can still eat it. This is because of their special teeth and powerful jaws. Wolverines have an upper molar in the back of their mouth. The molar is rotated sideways, towards the inside of the mouth. With these adaptations, the wolverine can tear off flesh, even from a solidly frozen carcass! They can crush and eat every hoof and bone of even the largest animal.

Check Your Understanding

1. *Molar* is to *tooth* as
  a. *wolverine* is to *weasel*.
  b. *wolverine* is to *carcass*.
  c. *wolverine* is to *hibernate*.
  d. *wolverine* is to *grizzly bear*.

2. From the context of the passage, you can infer that if a wolverine killed a large animal,
  a. it would have to eat it all at once.
  b. it could eat all but the bones and hooves.
  c. it could store it under the snow for later.
  d. it would only be able to eat it before it froze.

3. Wolverines are *not* native to
  a. Asia.
  b. Africa.
  c. Europe.
  d. North America.

4. Most likely, the wolverine
  a. has no fur.
  b. has spotted fur.
  c. has thin, short hair.
  d. has a thick coat of fur.

/4

Warm-Up
20

Name _____

Robot Pills

Think of a pill you can swallow. Think of a robot. Now, put the two together. Pill-sized robots are called mini bots. Mini bots are now being used in medicine. One mini bot called the M2A is a wireless camera pill. It is used to take pictures of a person's gastrointestinal tract. Other mini bots are guided by external magnets. Using magnets, doctors have more control over the bots' movements inside the body.

Some of the mini bots take pictures. Other bots deliver medicine. Other bots clip off bits of tissue. The tissue is used for a biopsy. A biopsy is when a bit of tissue is taken. The tissue is then examined. By examining the tissue, doctors try to figure out what is wrong.

Currently, scientists are working on developing mini bots for surgery. The plan is that a person will swallow a dozen or so mini bot pills. Once inside the stomach, the pills would combine with one another. They would form into a big, powerful robot. Surgeons would guide the robot wirelessly. After the surgery was completed, the mini bots would separate. The big, powerful robot would break apart. It would be nothing but a dozen or so mini bots that would be small enough to pass harmlessly out of someone's system.

Check Your Understanding

1. How are some of the mini bots being guided?
   a. by gas
   b. by magnets
   c. by electricity
   d. by solar power

2. What is the plan for getting big, powerful robots inside a person?
   a. A person would swallow them in about two pieces.
   b. A person would swallow them in about twelve pieces.
   c. A person would swallow them in about twenty pieces.
   d. A person would swallow them in about twenty-two pieces.

3. *Powerful* is to *weak* as
   a. *guide* is to *lead*.
   b. *combine* is to *mix*.
   c. *examine* is to *study*.
   d. *separate* is to *combine*.

4. What is it called when a doctor takes a bit of tissue to examine?
   a. a biopsy
   b. external surgery
   c. a wireless camera pill
   d. a gastrointestinal tract

/4

Name _____

Surprise at the Necropsy

The octopus was found on the floor. Somehow during the night, it had escaped from its tank in the aquarium. Octopi are escape artists, so its keepers knew to put a heavy lid on its tank. Still, the octopus had somehow squeezed through the tiny crack between its heavy lid and tank walls. It had become stranded on the floor. Without access to salt water, the poor creature had died.

The octopus was put in a plastic bag. The plastic bag was sealed. Then it was taken to pathologists at a university. Pathologists are doctors. They look for the causes, symptoms, or results of disease. The pathologists were going to do a necropsy on the octopus. A necropsy is when a dead animal is examined.

When the pathologists were ready to do the necropsy, they took the sealed bag with the octopus out of the refrigerator. Then they took the octopus out of the bag. They put it on the table. That's when they got a surprise. The octopus reached up and grabbed the arm of a pathologist! Needless to say, the doctor was very startled! What happened then? With a police escort and sirens blaring, the octopus was taken back to the aquarium!

Check Your Understanding

1. Most likely, the octopus was given a police escort because
   a. the octopus had scared the pathologist.
   b. people were afraid the octopus would escape.
   c. the seal on the plastic bag had been broken.
   d. the octopus needed to quickly get back in salt water.

2. The plural of *octopus* is *octopi*. What other word is listed with the correct plural?
   a. bus, busi
   b. cactus, cacti
   c. mouse, mouses
   d. window, windowi

3. The purpose of the passage is to
   a. describe what pathologists do.
   b. list different kinds of doctors.
   c. share a story about an animal escape artist.
   d. teach you what to do if an octopus grabs you.

4. What had been done to prevent the octopus from escaping?
   a. A heavy lid had been put on its tank.
   b. It had been put under police protection.
   c. It had not been given access to salt water.
   d. All the cracks in the tank walls had been sealed.

/4

Warm-Up

22

Name _____

The Disappearing Spoon

You pick up a teaspoon. It looks like an ordinary teaspoon. It feels solid. It weighs about the same as every other teaspoon you've ever used or picked up. You are drinking a hot **beverage**. It could be tea, coffee, cider, or chocolate, but it needs stirring. You dip your spoon into your steaming beverage and begin to stir. That's when you are shocked. That's when you can't believe what is happening. That's when your spoon disappears!

You have fallen for an old chemistry trick. Gallium is an element. An element is a substance that is made entirely from one type of atom. Everything in the world is made up of different combinations and mixtures of elements. Each element has particular traits and properties. Gallium is a liquid metal. It is solid at moderate room temperature, but it melts at 84°F. Gallium is easily molded. It looks like aluminum. In fact, it is one of the few liquid metals you can touch without boiling your finger to the bone.

Your disappearing spoon was nothing but molded gallium! When you immersed it in the hot liquid, it simply melted. It changed from a solid state into a liquid state.

Check Your Understanding

1. Which of the following is *not* true about gallium?
   a. It is safe to touch.
   b. It is easy to mold.
   c. It is always in a liquid state.
   d. It is made up of only one type of atom.

2. From the context of the passage, a **beverage** must be
   a. hot.
   b. cold.
   c. solid.
   d. liquid.

3. Water is made up of hydrogen and oxygen atoms. From this, you can infer that
   a. water is an element.
   b. water is not an element.
   c. elements cannot combine.
   d. gallium is one of the elements in water.

4. What would have happened if you had held the gallium spoon in your mouth?
   a. It would have started to melt.
   b. Nothing would have happened.
   c. It would have started to boil.
   d. It would have burnt your mouth.

/4

Warm-Up 23

Name _____

Extreme Flying

There is a bird that sees more daylight in a year than any other bird or animal. Add up the distance this bird flies in its lifetime, and it is equal to flying to the moon three times! The bird is the Arctic tern. The Arctic tern migrates every year. It breeds mainly on the shores of the Arctic Ocean. It breeds in the summer when the days are long. Then it flies to the other side of the world. It flies to Antarctica.

There was an airplane pilot flying over Ireland. He was at 27,000 feet. He looked out the window and spotted thirty whooper swans. The pilot radioed in what he was seeing. The birds' height was confirmed on radar by air traffic control. Bar-headed geese have been spotted flying even higher. They have been spotted flying over the Himalayas at altitudes approaching 29,500 feet.

There is a bird that went in search of food for its chick. The bird had been fitted with a miniature radio transmitter. Tracking by satellite showed that the bird was gone for thirty-three days! It flew 9,320 miles! The bird is the wandering albatross. It is no surprise that the wandering albatross holds the record for the longest recorded flight in search of food for its chick.

Check Your Understanding

1. From the context of the passage, a wandering albatross chick
   a. can survive for thirty-five days without food.
   b. can fly as soon as it hatches.
   c. is taken care of by at least one parent.
   d. does not need parents to survive.

2. Most likely, the Arctic tern is in Antarctica when it is
   a. winter there and the days are long.
   b. summer there and the days are long.
   c. winter there and the days are short.
   d. summer there and the days are short.

3. The purpose of the passage is to
   a. explain why birds migrate.
   b. talk about what birds eat.
   c. show how birds are tracked.
   d. describe amazing bird flights.

4. You are at 29,500 feet in the Himalayas. You spot a bird flying overhead. Most likely, you are seeing
   a. an Arctic tern.
   b. a whooper swan.
   c. a bar-headed goose.
   d. a wandering albatross.

/4

Warm-Up
24

Name _____

All About Nerves

Just suppose you could join all the nerves in your body from end to end. How far would all your nerves stretch? They would stretch about sixty-two miles! What are all these nerves for? Your nerves are made up of thousands of tiny threadlike fibers. The fibers are incredibly thin. They are less than 1/25,400th of an inch wide. The fibers are made up of billions of microscopic nerve cells.

Like a computer, nerve cells carry tiny electrical signals. The electrical signals transmit messages between the brain and other parts of the body. The information is transmitted at incredibly high speeds. The fastest nerve signals travel at more than

630 feet per second. This means that a nerve signal can go from your toe to your brain in less than 1/100th of a second!

Nerves may be small, but they are very complicated. If a nerve is damaged, it may never heal. (Contrast this to your skin that renews itself every month.) If a nerve does heal, it may take weeks or months. Damaged nerves may not be able to transmit messages from your brain to your muscles. You may become paralyzed, or unable to move.

Check Your Understanding

1. From the context of the passage, you can infer that you
   a. could see nerve cells with the naked eye.
   b. could not harm nerve cells in your toes.
   c. could run as fast as nerves can transmit messages.
   d. could not see a single nerve fiber with the naked eye.

2. Scientists studied squid nerves to help understand our own nervous system. One reason may be because
   a. squid nerve fibers are bigger.   c. squid nerve fibers are thinner.
   b. squid nerve fibers are smaller.   d. squid nerve fibers are more complicated.

3. A nerve signal can travel from your toe to your brain in
   a. less than 1/10th of a second.   c. less than 1/100th of a minute.
   b. less than 1/100th of a second.   d. less than 1/1000th of a second.

4. The purpose of your nerves is to
   a. travel fast.   c. transmit messages.
   b. renew itself.   d. paralyze your muscles.

/4

Warm-Up 25

Name _____

The Gutless Wonder

Go down to the bottom of the ocean floor. Go over a mile down. You see a bunch of white tubes. The tubes are made of a tough, natural material called *chitin*. All of a sudden, like a lipstick being opened, bright red plumes shoot out. You are seeing giant tubeworms. You are seeing gutless wonders.

Giant tubeworms can grow to eight feet tall. They can be as big around as your wrist. The giant tubeworms do not have mouths or eyes. They do not have a stomach or a gut. How can these gutless wonders eat? How can they survive on the dark ocean floor?

The tubeworms make their homes around hydrothermal **vents**. Hot chemicals and gases from inside Earth spew out of the vents. Inside the tubeworms there are billions of bacteria. The bacteria and the tubeworms depend on each other for survival. They have a symbiotic relationship. The tubeworm provides a stable home for the bacteria. The bacteria convert chemicals shooting out of the vents into food for the worm.

How did the bacteria get inside the gutless tubeworm? It was a mystery. What did scientists find out? They found that in the early stages of life, tubeworms had a mouth and a gut. Once the bacteria were inside, the mouth and the gut disappeared.

Check Your Understanding

1. Which of the following statements is true about the tubeworm?
   a. It can grow taller than your parent.
   b. It can be as big around as your neck.
   c. It grows a mouth in its later stages of life.
   d. It converts bacteria from the vents into food.

2. What is the tubeworm's tube made of?
   a. chalk
   b. chitin
   c. chestnut
   d. chocolate

3. Most likely, in a symbiotic relationship,
   a. animals live under the water to survive.
   b. one animal survives by eating other animals.
   c. animals live in a pack to help each other survive.
   d. two different animals depend on each other for survival.

4. A **vent** is
   a. a home.
   b. a plume.
   c. an opening.
   d. a chemical.

/4

Name _____

Why the Scientist Knew

A scientist had a young lab assistant. One day, the scientist was sitting in his office. Suddenly, the door was flung open and the excited lab assistant came charging in. He was holding up a glass flask with an oozing, bubbling green liquid in it. His voice trembling with excitement, the lab assistant cried, "I've done it! I've done it! It took days, nights, weeks, and months, but at last I've succeeded! It's a scientific miracle! I have created a universal solvent. It is an acid so strong that it is capable of dissolving all other substances!"

The scientist took one look at his assistant holding the glass flask with the oozing, bubbling green liquid and said, "You're wrong." The scientist knew that the solution in the glass bottle was not a universal solvent. His assistant may have worked hard, but he had not created a scientific miracle.

As his lab assistant began to sputter indignantly, the scientist cut him off with one question. The question was simple, but it proved that he was right. What was the scientist's question to his lab assistant? It was, "How are you holding it in a glass bottle?"

Check Your Understanding

1. What could *not* be true about the solvent the lab assistant made?
 a. It could dissolve gold.
 b. It could dissolve glass.
 c. It could dissolve silver.
 d. It could dissolve plastic.

2. How did the scientist come to his conclusion?
 a. by smelling
 b. by observing
 c. by experimenting
 d. by asking questions

3. *Flask* is to *bottle* as
 a. *purse* is to *bag*.
 b. *purse* is to *carry*.
 c. *purse* is to *books*.
 d. *purse* is to *straps*.

4. Which of the following words describe the lab assistant?
 a. excited and lazy
 b. grumpy and angry
 c. hardworking and eager
 d. indignant and successful

/4

Warm-Up

27   Meat-Eating Caterpillars

Name _____

Most people don't think caterpillars eat meat. They don't think of them as carnivores. They think of them as eating plant matter. They think of them as herbivores. Roughly, there are just over 160,000 known species of moths and butterflies. The majority of these are herbivores. Over 99 percent eat plant matter only, yet there is a small minority that is carnivorous. While in the caterpillar stage, they eat meat.

One carnivorous caterpillar lives on the Danish island of Laeso. It starts as a tiny white egg laid on a marsh gentian, a kind of flower. After the egg hatches, the caterpillar feeds on the flower for about two weeks. Then it drops to the ground where passing ants carry it into its nest. Why do the ants do this? The caterpillar smells the same as the ants' larvae do!

Once inside, the ants feed the caterpillar. The caterpillar takes what it is fed, but it also supplements its diet with meat. What is its meat source? It is the ants' own brood! The caterpillar remains in the nest feasting on the ants' young until it becomes a butterfly. Once it hatches, it quickly flees the nest. The cycle repeats itself when the butterfly lays its own eggs on a marsh gentian.

Check Your Understanding

1. What is the caterpillar's source of meat?
   a. the marsh gentian
   b. what the ants feed it
            c. the ants' brood or young
            d. the caterpillar's own eggs

2. From the context of the passage, which of the following answers is true?
   a. A deer is a carnivore.
   b. A shark is an herbivore.
            c. An eagle is an herbivore.
            d. An anteater is a carnivore.

3. What percent of caterpillars eat meat?
   a. 99 percent
   b. one percent
            c. less than one percent
            d. greater than one percent

4. *Majority* is to *minority* as
   a. *best* is to *worst*.
   b. *most* is to *least*.
            c. *oldest* is to *newest*.
            d. *hottest* is to *coldest*.

/4

Warm-Up
28

Name _____

Motion Sickness

You can call it "car sickness," "air sickness," or "sea sickness." It is all motion sickness. Motion sickness relates to our sense of balance. We feel motion sickness when different senses send conflicting messages to our brain. The messages may come from our inner ear, eyes, or sense receptors in our skin, muscles, and joints.

For example, you may be reading a book in a car. Your inner ear monitors the directions of motion, such as forward, backward, turning, side-to-side, up, and down. Your inner ear feels the car's movement. It sends messages to your brain about direction movement. It tells your brain where you are going. Your eyes, in contrast, tell your brain that you aren't moving. This is because the print in the book is not moving.

You may be inside an airplane. The plane may begin to be tossed around by air turbulence. Your eyes are telling your brain you aren't moving because the inside of the plane looks the same. Your inner ear is telling your brain something else. So are the sense receptors in your skin, muscles, and joints. This **conflict** in messages tells our brain that something is wrong, and consequently, we feel sick.

Check Your Understanding

1. You may feel motion sickness most in a
   a. plane that is flying level.
   b. boat that is on calm water.
   c. car on a curvy, windy road.
   d. car on a straight, flat road.

2. Sometimes, looking at something far away will help reduce car sickness. Most likely, this is because it helps to coordinate
   a. messages from your skin.
   b. signals from your eyes to your joints.
   c. messages from your muscles to your skin.
   d. movement signals from your eyes and inner ear.

3. Messages sent from what answer below don't matter when it comes to motion sickness?
   a. outer ear
   b. inner ear
   c. receptors in the skin
   d. receptors in the muscles

4. There is a **conflict** when something
   a. agrees with something else.
   b. goes against something else.
   c. sends messages to something else.
   d. receives messages from something else.

/4

Warm-Up
29

Name _____

An Impressive Crown

The Washington Monument is in Washington, D.C. It is tall and white. It is topped with aluminum. The monument was built to honor George Washington. It was meant to impress people. Why was it crowned with aluminum then? We see aluminum products all around us. Most of our soda cans are made of this metal. Aluminum doesn't seem special at all. If the monument was meant to impress us, why wasn't it topped with gold?

Aluminum is an element. It is the most **abundant** metal in Earth's crust. There is plenty of it, but in nature it is always combined with other elements to form compounds. At the time the Washington Monument was built, people didn't know an easy way to obtain pure aluminum.

The Washington Monument was finished and crowned in 1884. People were greatly impressed by its crown. Using aluminum to top it was more impressive than using gold. That's because, at that time, aluminum was much dearer than gold. Aluminum cost more. It was the most expensive metal in the world.

Over the years, chemists worked on ways to get pure aluminum. They worked on ways to extract it from compounds. One method was developed in 1886. It used an electric current to remove the oxygen from aluminum oxide. This method is still used today.

Check Your Understanding

1. What might be one reason the method used today wasn't invented until 1886?
   a. People had to run out of gold.
   b. People had to find aluminum compounds.
   c. People had to see the Washington Monument.
   d. People had to learn how to use electricity.

2. The Washington Monument was topped with aluminum so
   a. people would be honored.
   b. people would be impressed.
   c. people would spend a lot of money.
   d. people would feel an electric current.

3. Most likely, what happened to the price of aluminum after chemists learned how to extract it?
   a. The price went up.
   b. The price went down.
   c. The price stayed the same.
   d. The price was the same as the price of gold.

4. When something is **abundant**,
   a. it is an element.
   b. it is a compound.
   c. there is a lot of it.
   d. it can be obtained in a pure form.

/4

Name _____

Big Snakes

There are two enormous snakes. They are both constrictors. This means that they kill their prey by constricting it, or wrapping themselves around and suffocating it. One of the big snakes lays eggs. The other big snake does not lay eggs. Instead, it gives birth to live young. This fact is enough to tell you which snake could be an anaconda and which one could be a reticulated python.

Anacondas are a type of boa constrictor. Anacondas can grow up to 30 feet long and weigh as much as 280 pounds. Like pythons, boas have two lungs (most snakes have just one), but unlike pythons, boas give birth to live young. The longest reticulated pythons can grow up to 33 feet, while the heaviest can weigh 250 pounds.

If eggs get too chilled, they will not hatch. Python mothers coiled around their eggs will sometimes look like they are shivering, but they are protecting their eggs. They are contracting their muscles to raise the temperature around them. They can raise the temperature by a few degrees, but it takes a lot of energy. It may take the mother two to three years to gain back the weight she lost while shivering. The mother won't lay eggs again until she has regained her weight.

Check Your Understanding

1. Which of the following is *not* true about the anaconda?
   a. It has one lung.
   b. It suffocates its prey.
   c. It is a boa constrictor.
   d. It gives birth to live young.

2. If someone asks you what snake is the biggest in the world, what question would you have to ask them?
   a. Do you mean a boa constrictor?
   b. Do you mean by weight or length?
   c. Do you mean before or after it eats?
   d. Do you mean before or after it lays eggs?

3. From the context of the passage, you can infer that
   a. all pythons are boa constrictors.
   b. some pythons are boa constrictors.
   c. all anacondas are boa constrictors.
   d. all boa constrictors are anacondas.

4. The passage is mainly about
   a. boa constrictors.
   b. pythons and their eggs.
   c. why some snakes shiver.
   d. two large constrictors.

/4

From the Past

Name _____

Warm-Up 1 — The Painting That Rode in an Ambulance

The painting was at risk of being stolen. The time was the 1930s, and World War II was raging. The German Nazis were stealing precious artworks from museums and homes. One of the most famous paintings in the world needed to be saved from the looting. It had to be secreted away and kept hidden from the plundering thieves. The painting is known as the *Mona Lisa*. The *Mona Lisa* was painted by Leonardo Da Vinci. It is a portrait of Lisa del Giocondo. It was started in 1503 and finished in 1519.

The portrait was hanging in the Louvre. The Louvre is in Paris, France. Museum **curators** stripped the walls bare of the museum in order to save their art from looting. They shipped more than 400,000 pieces out of Paris. They secreted them away to castles, caves, and salt mines.

Special care was taken with the *Mona Lisa* because of its fame and value. The *Mona Lisa* was taken out of Paris in an ambulance. This was for disguise. The ambulance was sealed up to protect the painting from air and temperature change. The painting survived its trip, but the museum curator who rode in the back of the ambulance almost didn't! He nearly ran out of oxygen!

Check Your Understanding

1. What was the author's intent in writing the passage?
   a. to tell how a painting was saved
   b. to give a history of World War II
   c. to make people want to go to museums
   d. to describe what a painting looked like

2. A **curator** must be a(n)
   a. ambulance driver.
   b. artist who paints portraits.
   c. famous and valuable painting.
   d. person in charge of a museum.

3. From the context of the passage, you can infer that the *Mona Lisa*
   a. is a portrait of Leonardo Da Vinci.
   b. hangs in a museum in Germany today.
   c. might have been hidden in a castle.
   d. was the only piece of art that was saved.

4. *Disguise* is to *hide* as
   a. *seal* is to *open*.
   b. *loot* is to *steal*.
   c. *protect* is to *harm*.
   d. *start* is to *finish*.

/4

Name _____

The Year Without a Summer

Usually, summer is a time of warmth. It is a time when planted food crops can grow and **flourish**. It is a time of long daylight hours. In 1816, farmers in the eastern United States expected summer to be like every other summer. They expected to plant their crops. They expected their crops to flourish and to harvest food for the coming year.

Instead, summer never came. There was snow in early June. There was frost in July, August, and September. The sky remained dark during the day, and there was little sunlight. Plants could not grow, and the crops failed. Why was all this happening?

On April 10, 1815, a faraway volcano erupted. The volcano was called Mount Tambora, and it was in Indonesia. Thousands of people close by were killed, but the eruption also affected people around the world. This is because ash and dust were thrown over fifteen miles into the air. The dust entered Earth's stratosphere where wind currents spread it throughout the world. The ash cloud was thick enough to block much of the sun's light and warming rays. The eastern United States was not affected immediately, as it took time for the dust cloud to reach the Northern Hemisphere.

Check Your Understanding

1. The dust was thrown into Earth's second major layer of atmosphere. This is the
   a. mesosphere.
   b. troposphere.
   c. thermosphere.
   d. stratosphere.

2. When something **flourishes**, it
   a. erupts.
   b. dries up.
   c. does well.
   d. does poorly.

3. Why might you want to pay attention to world news?
   a. You can't be affected by what happens in the past.
   b. You can be affected by something that happens far away.
   c. You can't get ready for anything that is going to happen.
   d. You can't be affected by something that happens far away.

4. From the context of the passage, you can infer that the United States
   a. usually has snow in June.
   b. does not have any volcanoes.
   c. is in the Northern Hemisphere.
   d. has more farmers than Indonesia.

/4

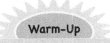

Warm-Up

3

Name _____

Long-Ago Manners

When George Washington was a schoolboy in Virginia, he copied something by hand. It was a list of 110 rules that had to do with etiquette. Etiquette has to do with manners, or how to behave politely in the company of others. Washington used the rules as a manners guide throughout his life. What are some of the rules Washington copied?

Rule #12 said, "Shake not the head, feet, or legs; roll not the eyes." It also instructed you to "bedew no man's face with your spittle by approaching too near him when you speak." Rule #13 said, "Kill no vermin, or fleas, lice, ticks, etc., in the sight of others. If you see any filth or thick spittle, put your foot dexterously upon it." (When you are *dexterous*, you are skillful and quick in the use of your hands, body, or mind.)

Many of the rules dealt with personal hygiene, but others dealt with how to treat people. For example, rule #1 said, "Every action done in company ought to be with some sign of respect to those that are present." Rule #6 said, "Sleep not when others speak, sit not when others stand, speak not when you should hold your peace, walk not on when others stop."

Check Your Understanding

1. What person needs to be acting dexterously?
   a. someone who is reading
   b. someone who is sleeping
   c. someone who is listening
   d. someone who is operating

2. Most likely, when Washington was living,
   a. more people made rules.
   b. more people went to school.
   c. more people used copy machines.
   d. more people had lice and fleas.

3. If you sleep when your teacher is talking, you are breaking
   a. rule #1.
   b. rule #6.
   c. rule #12.
   d. rule #13.

4. Which of the following answers is *not* proper etiquette today?
   a. giving your seat to an elder
   b. talking with your mouth full
   c. shaking with your right hand
   d. putting your napkin on your lap

/4

Name _____

The Dog Who Came Home

On a February day back in 1923, the Braziers' dog, Bobbie, appeared on their doorstep. It was mangy and scrawny. Its feet were cut and bleeding. The Braziers were pleased, but they were also astounded. How could it be possible? They had last seen their dog six months ago when they were vacationing in Wolcott, Indiana. The Braziers didn't live anywhere near Indiana. They lived in Silverton, Oregon!

The Braziers were heartbroken when they lost Bobbie. They had searched for him exhaustively. Bobbie was a Scotch collie and English shepherd mix. He had three unique scars. The Braziers knew it was their dog. Bobbie looked so worn that it looked as if he had walked the entire distance back home. Could that be possible?

Bobbie's feat of faithfulness was documented. People told when and where they had fed him and provided him shelter. People wanted Bobbie to become their dog, but Bobbie would always escape. Bobbie walked across eight states! He swam across rivers, including the ice-filled Missouri. He crossed deserts and the Rocky Mountains. Usually Bobbie moved in the right direction, but sometimes he ended up taking **detours**. The accidental detours added hundreds of miles to the trip. How far did Bobbie walk to get home in total? He traveled 2,800 miles!

Check Your Understanding

1. How long did it take Bobbie to make his way home?
   a. six years
   b. six months
   c. seven years
   d. seven months

2. When you take a **detour**, you
   a. turn in the right direction.
   b. take the shortest route possible.
   c. take a route through the mountains.
   d. turn aside from the direct or regular route.

3. From the context of the passage, you can infer that Bobbie got his scars
   a. after he escaped.
   b. after he got home.
   c. before he was lost.
   d. before he was the Braziers' dog.

4. Bobbie's coming home was called a "feat of faithfulness" because
   a. Bobbie never gave up.
   b. Bobbie had gotten lost.
   c. Bobbie stayed with other people.
   d. Bobbie's feet were cut and bleeding.

/4

Warm-Up
5

Name _____

Left to Burn

A house is on fire, and the fire brigade rushes to the fire. This is in Germany in 1680, so the firemen sit on a wagon pulled by horses. They have a flexible hose on their cart that was invented in 1672 by a man from the Netherlands. The firemen reach the house, and they see the flames. Do they stretch out their flexible hose and start dousing the flames? No, they do not. The house could have been saved, but instead the firemen drive away. The house burns to the ground.

There were no public fire services long ago. The government did not pay firefighters. People insured their buildings against fire through private companies. Insurance companies found that they saved money by putting out fires rather than allowing them to destroy buildings and what was inside. Each insurance company had its own private fire brigade.

Each insurance company had a special fire mark. The fire mark was a plate or plaque engraved with the name or emblem of the insurance company. The plaque was nailed to the buildings insured by the company. Usually, it was not on the ground floor, making it harder to mischievously remove. When a fire brigade showed up, it did not fight the fire unless the house was insured by its own company.

Check Your Understanding

1. The flexible hose was invented by a man from
   a. France.
   b. Germany.
   c. Iceland.
   d. the Netherlands.

2. When something is "plunged quickly into water," it is
   a. doused.
   b. insured.
   c. engraved.
   d. destroyed.

3. People still buy fire insurance today, so
   a. they can use an emblem.
   b. they can get help replacing what burned.
   c. firefighters won't leave their house to burn.
   d. the government won't have to pay firefighters.

4. From the context of the passage, a public service is one that
   a. pays insurance.
   b. has a special plaque.
   c. serves all the people.
   d. serves only those who pay.

/4

Name _____

Uncle Sam

Uncle Sam is a nickname. It is a nickname for the federal government. How did this nickname come about? One story about the origins of Uncle Sam goes back to the War of 1812. Only the federal government can declare war on another country. A state or city government cannot. The War of 1812 was between the United States and Great Britain. The war ended in 1815.

At that time, Samuel Wilson was a meat-packer in Troy, New York. The federal government awarded Wilson a contract. The contract was to supply beef for the troops. Cured beef was shipped from Wilson's plant in barrels. When Wilson was awarded his contract, all the barrels of beef that were to go to the troops were stamped with two big letters. The letters were "U" and "S."

Wilson was known locally as "Uncle Sam," so people said the "U.S." was for "Uncle Sam." As the barrels of beef were rolled and loaded at the plant, people would joke that it was "Uncle Sam's!" Soon, everyone, from near and far on the shipping path, would say that it was "Uncle Sam's." The truth is that "U.S." did not stand for "Uncle Sam" at all! The "U.S." stood for "United States"!

Check Your Understanding

1. Another title for the passage might be
   a. "Shipping Beef."
   b. "The War of 1812."
   c. "Feeding the Troops."
   d. "The Federal Nickname."

2. How long did the War of 1812 last?
   a. about three years
   b. about five years
   c. about thirteen years
   d. about fifteen years

3. The federal government might have a different nickname if
   a. the War of 1812 had lasted longer.
   b. more people had known Wilson's nickname.
   c. Wilson had not been awarded a contract.
   d. the letters on the barrel had been bigger.

4. *President* is to *federal government* as
   a. *beach* is to *lifeguard*.
   b. *mayor* is to *city government*.
   c. *state government* is to *governor*.
   d. *national park* is to *park ranger*.

/4

Warm-Up 7

Name _____

An Engineering Masterpiece

Back in the first century, the Roman Empire stretched into France. The Romans built something in the south of France that can still be seen today. Construction took almost twenty years. About 1,000 men worked on it. It allowed a city to grow. It was a true engineering masterpiece, and it still stands today. What could it be?

Romans needed a way to bring water to the city of Nîmes. They needed the water for their fountains and public baths. They needed it to flush waste through latrines and sewers. The Romans constructed an aqueduct called the Pont du Gard. The Pont du Gard stretches almost thirty miles from springs in Uzès all the way to Nîmes. It has three levels, and it stands 160 feet high. Water ran in a channel along its top level while a road ran along its bottom level.

The aqueduct was built of stones, some of which weighed six tons. The stones were carefully cut and fitted, and no mortar was used. The winch used to help lift the stones was a human-powered treadmill. The aqueduct only descended a total of forty feet over its entire distance. Gravity carried water to the city from the spring in less than thirty hours. This was a record-setting time for the first century.

Check Your Understanding

1. Which of the following statements about the Pont du Gard is *not* true?
a. It has three levels.
b. It is in the north of France.
c. It stands 160 feet high.
d. It stretches almost 30 miles.

2. From the context of the passage, you can infer that
a. cities can grow to any size.
b. cities need to have fountains.
c. the Romans built the first cities.
d. cities need a source of water to grow.

3. Which person is descending?
a. the one walking up a mountain
b. the one walking at record time
c. the one walking down a mountain
d. the one walking on level ground

4. From the context of the passage, the aqueduct might have been constructed
a. between 40 and 60 CE.
b. between 400 and 420 CE.
c. between 1400 and 1420 CE.
d. between 1600 and 1620 CE.

/4

Name _____

Seeing the Hidden Stomach

What if you have a stomach ache? Doctors have all sorts of tests they can do to see what is wrong. They can pass a thin, flexible, lighted tube down your throat. They can make images using X-rays, sound waves, or magnetic fields. Long ago, doctors knew very little about digestion. They didn't know how the stomach worked or how food was broken down. That all changed in 1822. This was well before doctors could do all the things they do now. What made learning about digestion possible?

In 1822, a man named Alexis St. Martin was accidentally shot in the stomach. No one thought he would live. St. Martin's wound was enormous, but it mostly healed. All that remained was a small opening leading into the stomach. The opening was covered by a fold of flesh that could be pushed aside.

Dr. William Beaumont was the doctor who treated St. Martin. While Beaumont was treating St. Martin, he learned all that he could about the "hidden" stomach. He extracted gastric juices. He observed food at various stages of digestion. He noted the stomach's muscular movements. Today, Dr. Beaumont is known as a founding father of gastric medicine. What about St. Martin? St. Martin lived with his stomach opening for over fifty more years!

Check Your Understanding

1. Why didn't Dr. Beaumont use X-rays to look at St. Martin's stomach?
   a. The wound never closed.
   b. St. Martin was too sick.
   c. X-rays weren't invented yet.
   d. St. Martin couldn't digest food.

2. Using words from the passage to help, choose the doctor that treats the stomach.
   a. neurologist
   b. pediatrician
   c. cardiologist
   d. gastroenterologist

3. Doctors can use all but what to make images of your stomach?
   a. pills
   b. X-rays
   c. sound waves
   d. magnetic fields

4. Dr. Beaumont was able to see as much as he did because St. Martin's wound
   a. had healed.
   b. had been so large.
   c. had come from an accident.
   d. had been looked at with a flexible tube.

/4

Warm-Up
9

Name _____

The First Speed Trap

Two police officers stood at their lookout posts. The lookout posts were camouflaged as dead tree trunks. The lookout posts were exactly one mile apart. One of the officers saw a car coming. The car appeared to be speeding. The officer pressed a stopwatch he was holding and phoned ahead to the officer in the other lookout. When the car passed the second lookout, the officer there consulted a speed-mileage chart.

According to the speed-mileage chart, the driver of the car was speeding. The officer that had consulted the chart then phoned ahead to a third officer. The third officer was manning a roadblock further down the road. When the car got to the roadblock, the third officer stopped the car. He gave the driver a ticket.

This happened in 1905. Just how fast was the car speeding? It was going a whopping twelve miles per hour! The driver had raced through an eight-mile-per-hour zone! Who was the driver of the speeding car? The driver was William McAdoo, the police commissioner of New York City! How did McAdoo feel about his ticket? He invited the officers to set up a similar device in New York City!

Check Your Understanding

1. How many police officers were a part of the speed trap?
   a. one
   b. two
   c. three
   d. four

2. How many miles per hour was McAdoo going over the limit?
   a. three
   b. four
   c. five
   d. six

3. How do you think McAdoo first felt when he was stopped at the roadblock?
   a. surprised
   b. delighted
   c. terrified
   d. frustrated

4. When the police officer consulted the speed-mileage chart, he
   a. pressed a stopwatch.
   b. gave the driver a ticket.
   c. made sure it was camouflaged.
   d. looked it over for information.

/4

Warm-Up 10

First Play, Then Invention

Name _____

There is a story about Rene T. H. Laennec and an invention. Laennec lived long ago in France. He was born in 1781 and died in 1826. Laennec was a doctor, and he needed to listen to a patient's heart. Laennec tried to do what he had been taught. He tried to use the percussion method. The percussion method used taps. A doctor would tap a patient's chest and listen for how it sounded. The percussion method didn't work for this particular patient, and Laennec was frustrated.

Laennec went for a walk and saw two boys with a long piece of wood. The boys were playing a game where one boy scratched the wood while the other held it up to his ear. The boys had great fun listening to the sounds coming through the wood. The boys' play led Laennec to wonder if he would hear chest sounds better if they were **amplified** through a hollow tube.

Laennec went back to his patient, and he listened to her heart through some rolled-up papers. Yes, the sounds were amplified, and he could hear her heart! Laennec experimented, and he found that sounds were clearer and louder if he listened through a hollow wooden tube. By first watching boys play, Laennec went on to invent the stethoscope!

Check Your Understanding

1. When something is **amplified**, it is
   a. invented.
   b. scratched.
   c. rolled up.
   d. made louder.

2. From the context of the passage, you can infer that the stethoscope was invented
   a. after 1821.
   b. after 1826.
   c. before 1781.
   d. before 1826.

3. What instrument is most likely in the percussion section of an orchestra?
   a. flute
   b. drums
   c. cello
   d. violin

4. What did Laennec use to listen to his patient's chest after seeing the boys play?
   a. wood
   b. paper
   c. cloth
   d. metal

/4

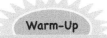

Name _____

11 How Banneker Saved the Capital

The United States of America was a young country. It had a temporary capital in New York. Then it had a temporary capital in Philadelphia. The Southern states felt that those cities were too far north. George Washington wanted to be fair. He decided to make a new capital. He chose a spot that was fair.

A French architect named Pierre-Charles L'Enfant planned the new capital. L'Enfant was excited. After all, most capital cities had just grown without being planned. With a new city, there could be a great plan. A magnificent city could be carved out of the marsh and trees. Three surveyors were chosen to help lay out the city boundaries. One of them was Benjamin Banneker. Banneker was a free black man. He only had a few years of school, but he had taught himself mathematics and astronomy.

At one point, L'Enfant ordered some homeowners to demolish their newly built homes. He didn't want the homes interfering with his plans. L'Enfant upset so many people that Washington had to fire him. In a rage, L'Enfant took the detailed map of the city with him. At first, people thought it was a catastrophe. They thought the plans were gone forever. Then Banneker stepped forward. The brilliant man simply reproduced the plans from memory!

Check Your Understanding

1. Which of the following is *not* true about Benjamin Banneker?
   a. He was French.
   b. He taught himself mathematics.
   c. He only had a few years of school.
   d. He helped lay out the capital's boundaries.

2. When you make a copy of something, you
   a. survey it.
   b. demolish it.
   c. reproduce it.
   d. interfere with it.

3. From the context of the passage, you can infer that Washington, D.C.,
   a. is a northern city.
   b. is not well planned.
   c. is a city that just grew on its own.
   d. is built over marshy ground.

4. *Temporary* is to *permanent* as
   a. *upset* is to *calm*.
   b. *demolish* is to *ruin*.
   c. *great* is to *magnificent*.
   d. *catastrophe* is to *disaster*.

/4

Warm-Up
12

Name _____

The Wall

In 1852, Augustus T. Dowd shot and wounded a bear. Dowd was supplying food for a Union Water Company labor crew. The Company provided water for California gold miners, and the crew was constructing water canals. Dowd tracked the bear about twenty miles into the unknown wilderness before deciding he would have to turn back. That's when he saw something. It was a wall.

Dowd couldn't believe his eyes. There were no settlements in the wilderness. How could there be a wall? As Dowd made his way up closer, his disbelief turned to amazement. Dowd wasn't standing in front of a wall. He was standing in front of a single tree! It was a giant redwood in a grove known today as the North Calaveras Grove.

Dowd convinced some of the men in the labor crew to follow him to the tree the next day. As the men got deeper and farther into the wilderness, they began to get angry. They were sure that Dowd was playing a trick on them. When they finally came upon the tree, the men were astounded. With its diameter of twenty-four feet, the tree measured about seventy-five feet around! It took five men more than three weeks to **fell** this tree.

Check Your Understanding

1. Why was Dowd so surprised that he was seeing a wall?
   a. He was in a grass clearing.
   b. He was expecting to see the wounded bear.
   c. He didn't know of any settlements in the area.
   d. The labor crew was building canals, not houses.

2. If a tree is **felled**, it is
   a. very big.
   b. cut down.
   c. standing.
   d. in a grove.

3. You might choose *not* to chop down such a big tree today so that others can
   a. be amazed.
   b. play tricks.
   c. track bears.
   d. mine for gold.

4. The passage is mainly about
   a. California.
   b. a water company.
   c. mining for gold.
   d. a redwood-tree sighting.

/4

Warm-Up
13

Name _____

The Great Molasses Flood

A boy and his sisters were walking home from school on January 15, 1919. They were in Boston, Massachusetts. They heard an explosive popping sound and a loud rumbling. Next, they were caught in a wave. The boy was picked up, tossed, and turned. Unable to breathe, he passed out. When he woke up, he discovered that he had been caught in a wave of molasses.

The popping sound was the sound of rivets, or metal bolts, exploding out of a tank. The tank was fifty feet tall with a diameter of ninety feet. The tank was filled with over two million gallons of molasses. Molasses was a standard sweetener in 1919. When the tank collapsed, the molasses swept into the streets like a black tidal wave. The initial wave was between eight and fifteen feet high, and it moved at a speed of thirty-five miles per hour. It lifted a train off its tracks and swept buildings off their foundations.

Horses and people were swept up in the wave. Twenty-one people were killed, and 150 were injured. The clean up was no easy feat. Salt water had to be pumped up from the harbor, and for months after, the streets remained tacky and sticky.

Check Your Understanding

1. What was molasses used as in 1919?
   a. a glue
   b. a drink
   c. a sweetener
   d. animal feed

2. From the context of the passage, you can infer that the initial wave of molasses
   a. moved faster than you could run.
   b. moved slower that you could run.
   c. was not deep enough to drown in.
   d. was not as sticky as salt water.

3. Most likely, the tank was made from
   a. wood.
   b. brick.
   c. stone.
   d. metal.

4. Which of the following words describes the clean-up task?
   a. simple
   b. difficult
   c. swift
   d. manageable

/4

Name _____

14   The Fruit That Wouldn't Sell

In 1804, some fruit was unloaded at New York's harbor. It was brought by John Chester, sea captain of the schooner *Reynard*. Chester had picked up the fruit in Cuba. He was hoping to make a profit off it. Instead, the fruit sat on the dock until it rotted. Not one person would buy it. The funny thing about the fruit that no one wanted is that today it is one of the most popular fruits in the United States. It is widely consumed around the world. What was the fruit that sat on the dock unsold and rotting?

It was the banana! Bananas originated in Southeast Asia over 2,000 years ago. They were brought to the Western Hemisphere in the early 1500s. Sailors who visited the tropics knew what to do with bananas, but other people didn't. More people were introduced to bananas as time went by. At first, bananas were thought to be so **exotic** and special that they were saved for special occasions. A banana might be given as a treat at a party or wedding banquet.

There is no such thing as a banana tree. Bananas grow on large plants without woody stems. A cluster of bananas is called a *hand*. Single bananas in a cluster are called *fingers*.

Check Your Understanding

1. Bananas could *not* have been grown in what country before the 1500s?
  a. India   c. Malaysia
  b. Mexico   d. South Africa

2. Which of the following words is an antonym for **exotic**?
  a. strange   c. ordinary
  b. foreign   d. different

3. The passage is mainly about
  a. party treats.   c. a sea captain.
  b. banana trees.   d. a widely consumed fruit.

4. If you saw a banana for the first time, you
  a. might try to eat it with the peel on.
  b. would think it was 2,000 years old.
  c. would know where it first originated.
  d. would know that it did not grow on a tree.

/4

Warm-Up

15

Name _____

The Trial

William "Duff" Armstrong was accused of murder. It didn't look good for the defense. There was an eyewitness who said he saw Armstrong and another man named James Norris strike the victim. Norris had already been found guilty. No one thought Armstrong's lawyer could win an acquittal.

The trial took place in 1858. The lawyer for Armstrong was a family friend. His name was Abraham Lincoln. Lincoln listened to the eyewitness. Over and over, the eyewitness said he was sure of what he had seen. He had seen the fight at 11:00 p.m. He had seen the victim being struck. He was some distance away, but the moon was shining brightly. There had been enough moonlight for him to see the crime take place.

Lincoln had the eyewitness repeat again and again that he was sure of what he had seen. The eyewitness repeated that he was sure because the moon had been shining so brightly. Then Lincoln brought forth a small, slim book. It was an almanac. The almanac was filled with astronomical information. The almanac proved that there would not have been enough moonlight to witness anything at the time and date of the crime. Armstrong was **acquitted**, and Lincoln went on to become the 16th president of the United States.

Check Your Understanding

1. From the context of the passage, you can infer that some of the astronomical information in the almanac must have been about
a. the moon's distance.
b. how bright the sun is.
c. what the moon is made of.
d. when the moon rises and sets.

2. When did the fight take place?
a. 11:00 p.m.
b. 11:00 a.m.
c. 12:00 p.m.
d. 12:00 a.m.

3. If someone is **acquitted**, he or she
a. will go to trial.
b. is an eyewitness.
c. is found not guilty.
d. has committed a crime.

4. Which of the following statements is true about Lincoln?
a. He was a family friend of Norris.
b. He became president after the trial.
c. He became a lawyer after he was president.
d. He defended Armstrong after he was president.

/4

Name _____

Two Invitations

The year was 1939. Eleanor Roosevelt was invited to a conference in Alabama. Roosevelt was the First Lady. She was the wife of President Franklin D. Roosevelt. The First Lady wanted to attend the conference, but where would she sit? At that time, black and white people could not sit together. It was the law. Roosevelt didn't like the law. She believed in equality for everyone. What did Roosevelt do? She had a chair put in the middle of the aisle. She sat between the separated sides!

That same year, Roosevelt issued her own invitation. It was to Miriam Anderson. Anderson was born in Pennsylvania. She was born in 1897. She was a wonderful singer. She had sung in capital cities around the world. She was going to sing in Constitution Hall in Washington, D.C. The Daughters of the American Revolution (DAR) owned the hall. The DAR said Anderson couldn't sing because she was African American.

Roosevelt was mad! Then she took action. She took action because, as she once said, "It's better to light a candle than to curse the darkness." What did Roosevelt do? She quit the DAR. She invited Anderson to sing on the steps of the Lincoln Memorial. Anderson sang on Easter Sunday. Over 75,000 people attended her concert.

Check Your Understanding

1. Where did Anderson sing on Easter Sunday?
   a. the steps of the White House
   b. the steps of Constitution Hall
   c. the steps of the Lincoln Memorial
   d. the steps of the Washington Monument

2. Think about where you can sit today. You can infer from the passage that
   a. laws can be changed.
   b. all laws are good laws.
   c. laws should never be changed.
   d. every state has the same laws.

3. *First lady* is to *president* as
   a. *king* is to *princess.*
   b. *duchess* is to *duke.*
   c. *prince* is to *crown.*
   d. *emperor* is to *ruler.*

4. Why did Roosevelt say, "It's better to light a candle than to curse the darkness"?
   a. She wanted people to stay mad.
   b. She didn't want the laws to change.
   c. She didn't like sitting in the dark, so she lit a candle.
   d. She believed you should try to make life better instead of just complaining about it.

/4

Warm-Up

17

Name _____

Ship Numbers

The *California* was a steamship. On October 6, 1848, it departed from New York Harbor, New York. Its goal was San Francisco, California. The ship carried six passengers and a cargo of mail. The aim of the voyage was to begin mail and passenger service between the two coasts.

The ship made its way past Cape Horn. Cape Horn is at the bottom of South America. The ship sailed up the west coast of South America and stopped in Callao, Peru. People there had already heard about the California gold rush. Hoping to strike it rich, sixty-nine Peruvians boarded the ship. The ship stopped again in Panama. More passengers squeezed on board. Now, the ship carried 350 passengers. The ship was only built to carry 200. It was so crowded that people were sleeping on the open deck. Everyone had to watch out for himself or herself.

On February 28, 1849, the *California* sailed into San Francisco. The passengers hailed small boats to ferry them across the harbor to the city. The captain was relieved to see the passengers depart. Now his boat wouldn't be overcrowded. After all the passengers left, what did the captain find? His crew was gone! They, too, had departed for the gold fields!

Check Your Understanding

1. Which pair of locations is mismatched?
   a. Peru, east coast
   b. Panama, west coast
   c. New York, east coast
   d. San Francisco, west coast

2. When you board a ship, you
   a. get on.
   b. get off.
   c. sail it.
   d. hail a ferry.

3. About how long did it take for the *California* to sail from New York to San Francisco?
   a. almost five weeks
   b. almost six weeks
   c. almost five months
   d. almost six months

4. What is true about the number of people on board the ship?
   a. More people got on board in Peru than in Panama.
   b. Fewer people got on board in Peru than in New York.
   c. Fewer people got on board in Panama than in New York.
   d. More people got on board in Panama than in New York.

/4

Warm-Up
18

Name _____

Second Only to Salt

When European explorers went to the New World, they tasted something new. They liked the taste so much that they brought back plants and seeds to their home countries. Today, people all over the world eat what was first grown in the Americas. The food is so popular that it is added to dishes all the time. Only salt is added more. It is so popular that packets of sauce made with it are taken on the space shuttle for the astronauts. What is this food?

The food is the hot pepper. Hot peppers come in all sizes, colors, and degrees of hotness. The hottest pepper is called the *Bhut Jolokia*, or ghost pepper. This pepper is so hot that, in some places, it is being rubbed on fence posts.

Why is it being rubbed on fence posts? It is being used to keep elephants away!

Hot peppers are hot because they contain a protein called *capsaicin*. Capsaicin has no taste, but when it touches nerve endings in your tongue, it sends a "pain" message to the brain. When the brain receives this "pain" message, it releases endorphins. Endorphins are the body's natural painkillers. (Endorphins are also produced when you exercise.) Drinking milk helps alleviate the burning sensation.

Check Your Understanding

1. The passage is mainly about
   a. food.
   b. peppers.
   c. explorers.
   d. endorphins.

2. Most likely, the packets of sauce on the space shuttle
   a. were tested on elephants.
   b. do not contain capsaicin.
   c. are not made from the ghost pepper.
   d. were brought back by European explorers.

3. Which of the following is true about endorphins?
   a. They alleviate pain.
   b. They produce a burning sensation.
   c. They can only be produced by exercise.
   d. They touch nerve endings in the tongue.

4. Which of the following countries is *not* a New World country?
   a. Chile
   b. Brazil
   c. Panama
   d. Germany

/4

Name _____

Warm-Up 19

The First Skyscraper

When the Great Chicago Fire struck in 1871, a large area of the city burned. Nearly one-third of its population was left homeless. That was almost 100,000 people! The city needed to rebuild. Land was expensive, so building up meant more people could be housed at less expense. Five stories were as high as anyone had gone before. Bricks and stones weighed too much to go any higher.

William Jenny was an architect. He was trying to design a building that was to have a "maximum number of small offices above the bank floor." Jenny wanted to go higher than five stories, but how? Frustrated at his failure to come up with a solution, he went home early. Surprised at his entry, Jenny's wife stood up. She placed the book she was reading on a birdcage. That's when Jenny came up with a solution to his design problem!

An interior framework, similar to a birdcage, would support the building. It would provide support like the skeleton of a mammal instead of the hard shell of a crab! Instead of heavy brick walls, light steel beams would support the building. People were amazed at Jenny's towering building when it was constructed. How high was Chicago's first skyscraper? It was nine stories!

Check Your Understanding

1. What type of person designs buildings?
   a. an engineer
   b. an architect
   c. an astronaut
   d. an archaeologist

2. From the context of the passage, you can infer that your weight is supported by
   a. your skin.
   b. your feet.
   c. your muscles.
   d. your skeleton.

3. What might be one reason why people hadn't come up with this design before?
   a. Cities hadn't burned before.
   b. Five-story buildings hadn't been built before.
   c. Steel mills hadn't been built before.
   d. Brick factories hadn't been built before.

4. Today, Jenny's skyscraper would be thought of as
   a. giant.
   b. small.
   c. towering.
   d. amazingly high.

/4

Name _____

A Daring Rescue

It was 1861, and The War Between the States was raging. The Confederate troops were advancing. Thaddeus Lowe was working for the Union. He was in the newly formed balloon corps. Lowe went up into the air in search of the Confederate soldiers. After spotting the enemy troops, Lowe began to descend over what he hoped was Union ground.

It was Union ground, but the soldiers didn't know what side Lowe was on! The Union soldiers yelled for Lowe to show his colors. Unfortunately, Lowe wasn't carrying a flag. The soldiers began to shoot at Lowe, and Lowe was forced to rise out of range. Then the wind pushed Lowe back over enemy lands! Lowe had no choice but to release the air in his balloon and crash land.

Lowe was saved in a daring rescue. Lowe's wife, Leontine, had been watching from the Union camp when the balloon went down. She helped soldiers track down Lowe. They had to be quiet and evade Rebel sentries. They found Lowe, but he was injured and the balloon was torn. Leontine left Lowe, but only to return as night fell. Dressed as a farmer, she drove a borrowed wagon. Under the cover of darkness, she loaded her husband and the balloon into the wagon and returned to safety.

Check Your Understanding

1. The Confederate soldiers were also
   a. shooting at Lowe.
   b. known as Rebel soldiers.
   c. known as Union soldiers.
   d. part of the balloon corps.

2. If you are asked to "show your colors," you are being asked to
   a. show your flag.
   b. start shooting.
   c. wait until night falls.
   d. search for enemy troops.

3. One reason Lowe returned to safety was because Leontine
   a. had a horse for Lowe to ride.
   b. had Lowe dress up as a farmer.
   c. had been able to mend the balloon.
   d. had seen where the balloon went down.

4. The passage is mainly about
   a. where the enemy line was.
   b. what soldiers wanted to see.
   c. what took place in the Balloon Corps.
   d. what caused the War Between the States.

/4

Name _____

Warm-Up 21

The Gold Miner's Diet

Gold miners flocked to California during the 1849 gold rush. The miners hoped to find riches. Instead, they found a monotonous diet. When something is *monotonous*, it is always the same. Miners mostly ate dried meat and dried beans. If they were lucky, they had flour and other dried foods. One miner wrote this about dried jerky: "When moistened and toasted, it will do something towards sustaining life; so also will the sole of your shoe."

Another miner wrote about getting scurvy. Scurvy is caused by lack of vitamin C, and it was quite common in miners. Animals can synthesize their own vitamin C, but people can't. People need to eat foods rich in vitamin C. Oranges, lemons, limes, tomatoes, potatoes, cabbages, and green peppers are all high in vitamin C.

The miner had bleeding, swollen gums and swollen limbs. His legs turned black as his blood vessels broke down. He was so weak that he couldn't walk. He wrote that he survived only because of an "accident-discovered **remedy**." The remedy came from some wild beans he found growing that he ate along with some spruce bark. The sprouts and bark gave him enough strength for him to make his way back to a camp where he could buy some potatoes.

Check Your Understanding

1. A **remedy** is
   a. a kind of bark.
   b. a type of dried meat.
   c. an accident or mistake.
   d. a kind of solution or answer.

2. What might be thought of as monotonous?
   a. shopping in different kinds of stores
   b. eating foods from different countries
   c. reading a mix of fact and fiction books
   d. listening to a song played over and over

3. What did one miner think about eating beef jerky?
   a. It was an accidental remedy.
   b. It was as good as eating a shoe.
   c. It helped you synthesize vitamin C.
   d. It kept your diet from being monotonous.

4. From the context of the passage, you can infer that vitamin C is found in all but
   a. a lime.
   b. an egg.
   c. a tomato.
   d. an orange.

/4

Name _____

The Man in the Mail

In 1849, Henry Brown thought of a way to escape from slavery. Brown was born a slave on a plantation near Richmond, Virginia. He had married and had children, but all his children had been taken away from him and sold. Brown decided he was going to mail himself to freedom.

Brown went to a storekeeper named James Smith. Smith didn't agree with slavery, and he said he would send Brown to a friend in Philadelphia, Pennsylvania. Brown and Smith then constructed a box with rough boards that measured two and a half feet deep, two feet wide, and three feet long. They lined the box with some cloth and drilled a few holes for **ventilation**. After Brown squeezed into the box, Smith nailed it shut. He addressed it to his friend and added the words "THIS SIDE UP: WITH CARE" to the label.

Unfortunately, no one paid attention to the label. As Brown was loaded from wagon, to steamer, to train, he was tossed and turned. At one point, he was upside down for so long that the veins in his head swelled up like thick ropes. Other times, people sat on the box and kicked at it. Despite the hard journey, Brown was successfully mailed to freedom. His trip took twenty-seven hours.

Check Your Understanding

1. Another title for the passage might be
   a. "Slave Life."
   b. "Mailed to Freedom."
   c. "The Importance of Labels."
   d. "Mail Time, Past and Present."

2. When something is **ventilated**, it is
   a. closed up.
   b. open to air.
   c. taken away and sold.
   d. constructed out of wood.

3. From the context of the passage, you can infer that Brown
   a. had to curl up in the box.
   b. could stand up in the box.
   c. had to lie flat in the box.
   d. could stretch out in the box.

4. How long did Brown's journey take?
   a. a little over one day
   b. a little over one week
   c. a little over a day and a half
   d. a little over a week and a half

/4

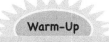

Warm-Up 23

Name _____

Silk as Armor

Most people think of silk as soft material or fine fabric. No one thinks of protective armor. However, long ago, silk was used as armor. Vests of silk were given to warriors to save their lives.

Genghis Khan was born in 1162 and was the ruler of the Mongolian Empire. By the time he died in 1227, he had conquered much of Asia. Genghis Khan was a fierce warrior. He and his conquering army were expert horsemen, and they could shoot their arrows with great accuracy while in the saddle. Genghis Khan had silk vests issued to his warriors. The vests were issued because they could save the lives of men hit by arrows.

How can a silk vest protect a warrior from an arrow? The vests were made of raw silk. Raw silk is rough and tough, with thick and thin strands woven together. As an arrow pierced a man's skin, the silk would not tear. Instead, it would neatly fold itself around the arrowhead and stay intact. This did two things. First, it made the arrow easier to remove because you could pull on the cloth. Second, if the arrow had been painted with poison, it helped keep the poison from spreading into the bloodstream.

Check Your Understanding

1. Genghis Khan might *not* have wanted heavy metal armor because
   a. he didn't need to protect himself.
   b. he wanted to conquer a lot of land.
   c. he spent so much time on horseback.
   d. he didn't think he could be poisoned.

2. Which of the following is *not* true about Genghis Khan?
   a. He died in 1227.
   b. He was born in 1162.
   c. He was an expert horseman.
   d. He conquered much of Africa.

3. When something is "sent or given out," it is
   a. armor.
   b. woven.
   c. issued.
   d. accurate.

4. *Arrow* is to *archer* as
   a. *cat* is to *string*.
   b. *horse* is to *saddle*.
   c. *baseball* is to *bat*.
   d. *puck* is to *hockey player*.

/4

Name _____

24   Why Sequoyah Wore a Turban

Sequoyah is a famous Cherokee. He was born in 1766 in Tennessee. He died in 1843. After seeing white men communicate with "talking leaves," Sequoyah invented the Cherokee writing system. There is a famous portrait of Sequoyah. In the portrait, he is holding up the letter symbols for his writing system. He is wearing a blue coat. He is wearing a turban on his head. Why is Sequoyah wearing a turban? How did that style begin?

A delegation of Cherokees went to England in 1730. They went to meet the king. The king's ministers met with the delegation first. The ministers looked at the Cherokees' tattoos. The ministers thought the Cherokees looked too frightening to meet the king. The ministers wanted the people in the delegation to cover up their tattoos.

The ministers gave the Cherokees clothes to wear for the royal audience. They gave them jackets. They gave them turbans. Some say that the clothes had been left behind by a delegation from India. When the delegation returned, they brought the clothes with them. The style of the clothes caught on. Soon, other Cherokees were wearing jackets and turbans. For many Cherokees, the turban became part of their cultural dress.

Check Your Understanding

1. The "talking leaves" Sequoyah saw were, most likely,
   a. messages on paper.   c. messages from India.
   b. messages on leaves.   d. messages from England.

2. From the context of the passage, you can infer that Sequoyah
   a. went with the delegation to England.
   b. was born after the delegation went to England.
   c. was born before the delegation went to England.
   d. communicated with the delegation that went to England.

3. Where was Sequoyah born?
   a. India   c. Indiana
   b. Texas   d. Tennessee

4. *Shoe* is to *foot* as
   a. *turban* is to *hat*.   c. *turban* is to *head*.
   b. *turban* is to *king*.   d. *turban* is to *clothes*.

/4

Warm-Up
25

Name _____

Two Anecdotes

An anecdote is a short, interesting, or amusing story. An anecdote is about a happening or a person. Alexander the Great was a Greek king. He lived from 356 to 323 BCE. Alexander set out to conquer the world. At one point, his empire stretched across three continents. Many anecdotes about Alexander have been told over time.

One anecdote is about Alexander and his horse. When Alexander was just ten years old, there was a horse that no one could tame or even mount. Being very observant, Alexander noticed something that no one else did. Alexander observed that the horse was afraid of his shadow. Alexander tamed the horse by turning it so it couldn't see its shadow.

Another anecdote is about a famous knot. The knot was called the Gordian knot. It was said that whoever could untie the Gordian knot would become king. No ends were visible on the knot. Many people had tried to untie the knot, but they had all failed. Just like everyone else, Alexander couldn't begin to untie the knot because he couldn't find its ends. Alexander didn't give up, though. Instead, he picked up his sword. With one stroke, he cut the knot in half! He then untied it with the **revealed** ends.

Check Your Understanding

1. What might be an anecdote?
   a. the age of your pet
   b. the name of your pet
   c. the color of your pet
   d. a story about your pet

2. When something is **revealed**, it is
   a. shown.
   b. hidden.
   c. untied.
   d. knotted.

3. What does the passage about the knot tell you about Alexander?
   a. He gave up easily.
   b. He wanted to be like other people.
   c. He didn't let problems stand in his way.
   d. He believed there was only one way of doing things.

4. From the context of the passage, you can infer that the first time Alexander saw his horse
   a. it was rainy.
   b. it was sunny.
   c. it was foggy.
   d. it was cloudy.

/4

Name _____

Don't Be Late!

Long ago in ancient Greece, Athens was a democracy. It did not have a king or queen. Instead, all male citizens could have a say in the running of the city. Each male citizen had one vote. A rich man's vote counted as much as a poor man's vote. Important matters were debated and voted upon at the assembly. There had to be a minimum of 6,000 people present for an assembly to take place.

Think about starting times. Sometimes events start late because people are tardy. People are slow to get going, or people think, "I'll just finish what I'm doing before I go." An assembly needed 6,000 people. If everyone was tardy, it might not start for hours! It would take forever to debate and decide important matters!

The ancient Athenians had a solution. The solution was red paint. The red paint was made from pigments that came from naturally tinted clay. Whenever an assembly was to take place, shops were forced shut. Then slaves would sweep the area with ropes dipped in red paint. If anyone **loitered** instead of moving to the assembly area, they would run the risk of having their clothes stained with the red paint. The red paint stains were permanent, and people caught wearing paint-stained clothes were fined.

Check Your Understanding

1. The passage is mainly about
   a. how an ancient democracy worked.
   b. where people met in ancient Greece.
   c. stores in the ancient city of Athens.
   d. how paints were made in ancient times.

2. If someone is **loitering**, he or she is
   a. tardy.
   b. moving quickly.
   c. speeding away.
   d. just hanging around.

3. Who could *not* vote in ancient Athens?
   a. a male citizen
   b. a rich man
   c. a poor man
   d. a rich woman

4. Most likely, people did *not* wear paint-stained clothes because
   a. they didn't want to debate.
   b. they didn't want to pay a fine.
   c. the paint was permanent.
   d. the pigments came from clay.

/4

Warm-Up

27

Name _____

Shopping Without Money

You are going shopping in ancient Egypt. You go to a large market in Thebes or Memphis. Goods abound, and there are many things to choose from. There are colorful vases, beautiful statues, and other detailed carvings made from stone, wood, metal, or ivory. There are clothes made out of the finest linen. There are baked goods, including thirty different types of bread. There is local produce, including pomegranates, melons, olives, dates, and figs. There are also exotic goods brought in from neighboring countries.

Local or exotic, when it comes time to pay, you will not use money. This is because when you go shopping in ancient Egypt, you don't pay with money. Instead, you barter. For example, you may trade fig cakes for a gold bracelet or sandals for a necklace.

Bartering in ancient Egypt took longer than using money, as the price had to be worked out, but the system worked well. Merchants were well trained, and they knew the prices of their goods in terms of other goods. What if you felt you were being given an unfair price? You could always call upon a market official. Market officials were always on hand to settle any arguments or disputes between traders.

Check Your Understanding

1. Bartering is a form of
   a. work.
   b. trade.
   c. study.
   d. linen.

2. When something is "strange or from a different land," it is
   a. local.
   b. exotic.
   c. ancient.
   d. stunning.

3. The passage is mainly about
   a. settling disputes.
   b. buying goods with money.
   c. bartering in ancient Egypt.
   d. life in Thebes and Memphis.

4. Why does it take longer to barter than to pay with money?
   a. Merchants are not very well trained.
   b. There are so many goods to choose from.
   c. Traders have to wait for market officials.
   d. The price has to be worked out in terms of other goods.

/4

Name _____

The Hidden Medals

Niels Bohr was sent two gold medals for safekeeping. They were Nobel Prize medals, which are very valuable. Nobel prizes are only awarded once a year. Getting a medal is a great honor. In many cases, you are awarded a medal if your research has led to scientific breakthroughs.

The medals were given to Bohr because Bohr was in Denmark. World War II was being fought. The two scientists who had been awarded the medals were afraid that the German Nazis would take their medals and use the gold. The scientists thought that Bohr could keep the medals safe in Denmark. Bohr took the medals, but then he realized they weren't safe. The Nazis were going to invade Denmark. Bohr didn't want to bury or hide

the medals because the two scientist's names were engraved on them. If the Nazis found the medals, the Nazis would know whom they belonged to. What could Bohr do to keep the medals safe?

The Nazis did indeed come searching. They never found the medals despite a complete and careful search. That's because a chemist named George de Hevesy came up with the **solution**. De Hevesy dissolved the medals in acid! The gold was hidden in a black **solution**. After the war, the gold was removed from the solution, and the medals were reforged.

Check Your Understanding

1. From the context of the passage, you can infer that Niels Bohr
   a. trusted the German Nazis.
   b. trusted George de Hevesy.
   c. didn't trust George de Hevesy.
   d. didn't trust Nobel Prize winners.

2. What was the gold dissolved in?
   a. tar
   b. acid
   c. water
   d. silver

3. Most likely, when the medals were reforged,
   a. World War II was still going on.
   b. it was no longer an honor to get a medal.
   c. the scientists' names were engraved on them.
   d. the medals were given to Niels Bohr as an award.

4. From the last paragraph, you can infer that **solution** could mean
   a. a mixture or a medal.
   b. a mixture or a search.
   c. an answer or a mixture.
   d. an answer or a question.

/4

Name _____

Warm-Up 29
Chained Shoes

There was a time when people chained their shoes. They didn't chain their shoes to keep them from getting stolen. They chained them to keep them from dragging! The chains ran from the shoe's toe to the wearer's knee. When and why would a chain be needed to keep shoes from dragging?

Long, pointy shoes were introduced to the English court in the 1300s. The shoes were worn by visiting Polish nobles. The English had never seen such shoes before, but the style took off. Whalebone was used to shape the shoes, and the toes were stuffed with hay, wood, or moss. Chains were sometimes used to keep the tips up.

The shoes were mostly worn by the very wealthy, as their length made it difficult to walk or work. At one point, Edward III, the king of England, made rules about shoe length. Edward could wear shoes of any length he wanted, but noblemen couldn't have shoe tips that measured over twenty-four inches. Gentlemen couldn't have shoe tips that measured longer than twelve inches. Common people couldn't have shoe tips that measured longer than six inches. It is said that this fashion became less popular after a certain duke was harmed because the length of his shoes kept him from fleeing from his attackers!

Check Your Understanding

1. After the king made his rule, someone was wearing shoes with tips that measured over twenty-six inches. Most likely, the person was
   a. a king.
   b. a nobleman.
   c. a gentleman.
   d. a common man.

2. The long, pointy shoes became popular in England
   a. after French nobles visited the court.
   b. after Polish nobles visited the court.
   c. before French nobles visited the court.
   d. before Polish nobles visited the court.

3. The passage is mainly about
   a. a shoe fashion from long ago.
   b. English fashion.
   c. rules kings make.
   d. a history of shoes.

4. From the context of the passage, you can infer that, most likely,
   a. noblemen were expected to work more than gentlemen.
   b. common men were expected to work more than noblemen.
   c. noblemen were expected to work more than common men.
   d. gentlemen were expected to work more than common men.

 /4

Name _____

Warm-Up 30 — What Chipped China Led To

Josephine Cochran was born in Shelbyville, Illinois, in 1839. Cochran had some china that had been in her family since the 1600s. Cochran greatly valued her seventeenth-century china. The dishes were very precious to her, but they were also a source of worry. Cochran didn't want the dishes broken or damaged. She didn't want them **marred** in any way.

Cochran was wealthy and had servants. The problem was that her servants were constantly chipping the dishes when they washed them. At one point, Cochran was so angry that she dismissed her servants and said she would wash the dishes herself. That's when she found out how hard it was to wash a dinner party's worth of dishes. Cochran knew there had to be a better way. She decided that if no one else would invent a machine to wash dishes, then she would.

Cochran worked out a design that was powered by a motor or a foot pedal. It employed water jets. It included a dish rack that kept the soiled dishes in place. It kept her plates, cups, and saucers from chipping because they couldn't knock against each other. Cochran received a patent for her machine in 1886. At first, Cochran's machine was mainly bought by hotels and restaurants.

Check Your Understanding

1. Which of the following years is in the seventeenth century?
a. 1586
b. 1672
c. 1783
d. 1825

2. What did Cochran find out when she washed her own china?
a. The best way to wash dishes was by hand.
b. It was hard to knock a cup against a plate.
c. Washing dishes was harder than she thought.
d. Her servants were chipping the dishes on purpose.

3. The passage is mainly about
a. an invention.
b. Shelbyville, Illinois.
c. where Cochran's china came from.
d. how Cochran treated her servants.

4. If you **mar** something, you
a. dismiss it.
b. employ or use it.
c. design or make it.
d. hurt or spoil its looks.

/4

Did You Know?

Name _____

Dog in the Bathtub

The house was on fire! The house was located in Farmingville, a small Long Island city in New York. It caught fire in October 2007. As the house filled with flames and smoke, no one thought the dog trapped inside could survive. The dog was a three-year-old Newfoundland named Jackson. Jackson was big and black and weighed about 130 pounds.

When firefighters burst through the smoke into the bathroom, they found Jackson. The dog was too terrified to move, but it was alive. How could Jackson be alive? How could he have survived in the smoky air? Jackson had jumped into the bathtub and had somehow pulled the curtain shut. Then he had lowered his snout as far as he could by the drainpipe. Jackson survived by breathing air that he was sucking up from the drain.

The firefighters were **astounded** when they found Jackson. They had been trained to duck down out of smoke if they ran out of oxygen and to look for air wherever they could find it. No one had trained Jackson, but nevertheless, the dog had figured out what to do. The firefighters joked about Jackson's training. The firefighters said that Jackson "actually sucking air out of the drainpipe" was "an old-school thing that a fireman would do."

Check Your Understanding

1. Which of the following is *not* true about Jackson?
a. He had been trained.
c. He was a Newfoundland.
b. He was big and black.
d. He was three years old.

2. From the context of the passage, which is the best synonym for **astounded**?
a. burnt
c. amazed
b. scared
d. terrified

3. You should crawl as low to the ground as possible when exiting a smoky building. Most likely, this is because
a. there will be no oxygen down low.
c. there will be less oxygen down low.
b. there will be more oxygen up high.
d. there will be more oxygen down low.

4. The passage is mainly about
a. how dogs get air.
c. how firefighters are trained.
b. how a dog survived a fire.
d. how a house in New York was on fire.

/4

Name _____

Warm-Up

2   A Boot That Is Not a Shoe

What do you think of when you hear the word "boot"? Do you think of a heavy shoe, or do you think of a car? What you think of may depend on where you live. American and British people may all speak English, but different words have different meanings.

In the United States, a *boot* is a type of footwear. In England, a *boot* is also the word used for the trunk of a car. A *bonnet* is a car's hood. Trucks are known as *lorries*, and all automobiles and other motor vehicles run on *petrol* (gas). The identifying plates on motor vehicles are called *number plates* rather than *license plates*.

In England, people call the last letter of the alphabet "zed" instead of "z." They take *lifts* instead of *elevators*. When waiting, they stand in a *queue* instead of a *line*. Babies are pushed in *prams* (baby strollers) by their *mum* or *mummy* (mom or mommy). Babies wear *nappies* (diapers), and when a baby cries, he or she may be given a *dummy* (pacifier) to **soothe** him or her. A cut or wound is covered with a *plaster* (Band-Aid®).

Potatoes are potatoes on both sides of the ocean, but when they are fried, the names differ. Americans have *potato chips* and *French fries*, while the English have *crisps* and *chips*.

Check Your Understanding

1. If you are told to "get in the queue," you should
  a. get in line.
  b. open the trunk.
  c. put on a bonnet.
  d. take the elevator.

2. What can you conclude from the passage?
  a. All words have more than one meaning.
  b. Crisps are not the same as potato chips.
  c. A word's meaning may depend on where it is used.
  d. American English is better than British English.

3. If you **soothe** something, you
  a. push it.
  b. fry potatoes.
  c. sail on the ocean.
  d. make it feel better.

4. The passage does *not* tell you
  a. what a plaster covers.
  b. why the meanings of the words changed.
  c. what identifies motor vehicles.
  d. word differences between the United States and England.

/4

Warm-Up 3

Name _____

When a Submarine Was an Iron Fish

World War II started in 1939. It lasted until 1945. It was an event that ended over sixty-six years ago, but it helped to shape the world we live in today. A secret code helped shape the outcome of the war. The code belonged to the Americans. Only a few Americans knew the code. Some of the code messages were intercepted, but still, they could not be deciphered. The code was unbreakable. The code talkers never talked about the code. They were asked not to. Even after the war, they kept silent. People didn't know about the code until much later. Who were these code talkers? What was the code that no one could decipher?

The code talkers were Navajo soldiers. The Navajo language was only spoken by the Navajo people. It had no written language. It is incredibly complex. Navajo recruits memorized the code and practiced sending and receiving messages. Before the code talkers, it would take a machine half an hour to encode a three-line message in English. The code talkers did it in twenty seconds!

At times, Navajo words needed to be used for English ones. For example, a submarine was an iron fish. A battleship was a whale. A plane was a bird, and America was "our mother." The country of Britain was "between waters."

Check Your Understanding

1. From the context of the passage, you can infer that code talkers
   a. had to work alone.
   b. had to work in pairs.
   c. had to work in a plane.
   d. had to work in a submarine.

2. A Navajo word for an animal was used for the word *army tank*. Most likely, what word was used.
   a. cheetah
   b. kangaroo
   c. tortoise
   d. panda bear

3. Another title for the passage might be
   a. "Code Talkers."
   b. "Intercepted Messages."
   c. "Learning to Speak Navajo."
   d. "How an Event Shaped the World."

4. When something is "translated from code into ordinary language," it is
   a. sent.
   b. encoded.
   c. received.
   d. deciphered.

/4

Name _____

The State Bird That Isn't

Every state has a state bird. Texas's state bird is the mockingbird. There is another animal that is jokingly referred to as "The Texas State Bird." This animal is not an avian creature at all. It is an insect! It is the mosquito.

Texans aren't the only ones with hordes of mosquitoes. Only one place in the world is free of them. What is this place? It is Antarctica. Mosquitoes may be small, but they cause great harm. This is because they are vectors, or carriers, of disease. They spread diseases like malaria and yellow fever.

Mosquitoes can't see well. They find their victims by honing in on exhaled carbon dioxide and body odors. They hone in, too, on temperature and movement. Contrary to what most people believe, mosquitoes

do not feed on blood. They feed on flower nectar and plant juices. Only the female mosquito will suck blood from a host. The blood is necessary for egg development. Male mosquitoes don't have the necessary mouthparts for blood sucking. Mosquitoes prefer horses, cattle, and birds to people.

Fortunately for Texans, their official avian state bird eats the insect "state bird." Bats and dragonflies help keep the mosquito population down, too. Just one bat can eat 1,200 mosquitoes in an hour!

Check Your Understanding

1. Texans may jokingly call mosquitoes their state bird because
a. they don't like mockingbirds.
b. the state has lots of cattle.
c. they are vectors for disease.
d. there are so many mosquitoes.

2. Which of the following is an example of an avian creature?
a. a dog
b. a hawk
c. a snake
d. an elephant

3. If you want to stop disease from spreading, you need to think about
a. staying away from the disease's vectors.
b. the name of the disease.
c. exhaling carbon dioxide.
d. how you feel when you are sick.

4. A mosquito may hone in on all but what?
a. color
b. movement
c. body odor
d. temperature

/4

Warm-Up 5

Name _____

Fallacies

What is a fallacy? A *fallacy* is a false or mistaken idea. There are some common fallacies when it comes to animals. A common fallacy about elephants is that elephants drink through their trunks. The facts are quite different. An elephant's trunk is its nose. You can't drink through your nose, and an elephant can't either. Elephants draw water up into their trunks. Then they squirt the water into their mouths or wherever else they want.

A second fallacy is about ostriches, the largest flightless bird in the world. Many people think that ostriches will bury their heads in the sand to hide. The facts are quite different. Just like you, an ostrich will suffocate if it buries its head in the sand. Some ostriches are over eight feet tall and weigh more than 250 pounds. Ostriches can run fast, and with their strong legs for kicking, there is little reason for them to hide in the sand.

Another fallacy concerns camels. Camels, both the one-humped Dromedary and the two-humped Bactrian, don't use their humps to store water. Their humps are used to store fat, and they aren't even hollow. A poorly fed camel's hump will be shrunken and small. It may even flop from side to side. On the other hand, a well-fed camel's hump is large and firm.

Check Your Understanding

1. Which of the following statements is true?
   a. A camel's height is given in the passage.
   b. An elephant's weight is given in the passage.
   c. Two types of camels are named in the passage.
   d. An ostrich's hiding place is named in the passage.

2. Most likely, if you want to buy a camel, you
   a. want one with a floppy hump.
   b. don't care what its hump is like.
   c. want one with a hump that is large and firm.
   d. want one with a hump that is shrunken and small.

3. From the context of the passage, you can infer that people
   a. don't always know the facts.
   b. never have their facts straight.
   c. always have their facts straight.
   d. don't care if they know the facts.

4. *Fallacy* is to *truth* as
   a. *fast* is to *speedy*.
   b. *large* is to *enormous*.
   c. *common* is to *ordinary*.
   d. *shrunken* is to *swollen*.

/4

Name _____

Warm-Up

6

Air Force One

An air traffic control officer uses the words "Air Force One." This can mean only one thing. It means that the president of the United States is on board an aircraft. People usually think of *Air Force One* as one of two Boeing 747 jets. The call sign, though, is used for any aircraft the president is on.

When and why did the call sign "Air Force One" come about? In 1953, President Eisenhower was on *Air Force* 8160. His call sign was 8160. Eastern Airlines Flight 8160 accidentally entered into the president's airspace. Flight 8160's call sign was the same as the president's! For security reasons, a call sign just for the president was developed.

Each of the two Boeing 747 jets in the president's fleet has a large office for the president. Each has a bedroom. Each has a gym and shower room, too. There is a large conference room. There is even an operating room. There are two large **galleys**, and kitchen staff can prepare up to one hundred meals at once. Freezers are stocked with at least one week's worth of meals. For safety reasons, the plane can refuel in the air. It has its own retractable steps so it does not have to rely on local airports. Secret Service men are hidden throughout the plane.

Check Your Understanding

1. If an air traffic controller uses the call sign "Air Force One,"
   a. it is before 1953.
   b. the president must be on his Boeing 747.
   c. a plane entered the president's airspace.
   d. the president is on an aircraft in the air.

2. Which of the following animals can retract its head, just like the steps on *Air Force One*?
   a. a rabbit
   b. a turtle
   c. a lizard
   d. a giraffe

3. From the context of the passage, you can infer that the president
   a. can't work while flying.
   b. has to rely on local airports.
   c. can stay in the air for a week.
   d. will need the plane to land if he needs an operation.

4. A **galley** is a plane's
   a. kitchen.
   b. freezer.
   c. shower room.
   d. operating room.

/4

Warm-Up
7

Name _____

Painted Food

The hamburger looks delicious. It is a deep, rich brown, and it is resting on a fresh, plump bun dotted with sesame seeds. The image makes you want to bite right into the juicy burger. The hot fudge sundae is covered in thick syrup and mounds of whipped cream. The image of the **delectable** treat makes your mouth water. All you want to do is feast; or do you?

Food advertisers have tricks of the trade. The bottom line is that food advertisers want you to buy their products. People are more likely to feel hungry and spend money if the food is presented in a mouth-watering fashion. Food can't stand up to hours under hot lights while it is being photographed. In real life, food is messy. It gets soggy, discolored, or it melts.

Hamburgers are painted with brown food coloring. After the seeds on the bun are glued in place, the bun is sprayed with a waterproof solution to keep it from getting soggy. Real ice cream has to be used in ice cream ads, but ads for whipped cream or syrup can use artificial ice cream. Artificial ice cream is made from shortening, powdered sugar, corn syrup, and food coloring. It can be kept in a plastic bag for months, and it never melts!

Check Your Understanding

1. The passage is mainly about
   a. artificial ice cream.
   b. why hamburgers are so tasty.
   c. some advertising food tricks.
   d. food that gets soggy or melts.

2. Most likely, if you see an ad for food,
   a. there is nothing artificial about it.
   b. the food would taste as good as it looks.
   c. something has been done to make it look better.
   d. it would look exactly the same if you cooked it.

3. A synonym for **delectable** is
   a. amazing.
   b. tasty.
   c. disgusting.
   d. average.

4. Why might a chicken be filled with paper towels before it is photographed?
   a. to dry out the inside and to make it smell
   b. to waterproof it and to stop it from melting
   c. to stop it from leaking and to make it taste better
   d. to make it plumper and to make the paper towels steam when cooked

/4

Warm-Up 8

Name _____

When Ghoti = Fish

English spelling is not logical. It often doesn't make sense. George Bernard Shaw was a famous playwright. Shaw once said that if English spelling was logical, the word *fish* would be spelled *ghoti*. What was Shaw's reasoning? What's the logic behind his statement?

Think of the word *enough*. Think of what the "gh" sounds like in that word. It sounds like the "f" in *fish*! *Tough* and *rough* are other examples of words where the "gh" makes the *f* sound. Now think of the word *women*. When you pronounce *women*, the "o" sounds like a short *i*. It sounds like the short *i* in *fish*!

You may be thinking that Shaw can build a case using letter sounds from the words *enough* and *women*, but how can "ti" make the *sh* sound in *fish*? Think of the word *ambitious*. If you are ambitious, you have ambition. You have great hopes and aims. When you pronounce the word *ambitious* correctly, the "ti" sounds like the *sh* in *fish*! The "ti" sounds like *sh* in the word *fictitious* (*fictitious* means that it is made up, or fiction), also. Using Shaw's logic, the correct pronunciation of *ghoti* would indeed be *fish*!

Check Your Understanding

1. From the context of the passage, you can infer that spelling is hard because
   a. letters never sound the same in different words.
   b. letters always sound the same in different words.
   c. letters rarely sound the same in different words.
   d. letters don't always sound the same in different words.

2. Someone writes *pheel* instead of *feel*. Someone could use all but what word to say their spelling was logical?
   a. phone
   b. person
   c. phantom
   d. elephant

3. *Fictitious* is to *real* as
   a. *bad* is to *evil*.
   b. *huge* is to *large*.
   c. *tiny* is to *small*.
   d. *strong* is to *weak*.

4. In which of the following words does the "c" sound different?
   a. cape
   b. city
   c. cause
   d. comfortable

/4

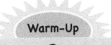

Warm-Up 9

Name _____

What the Folding Chair Became

On June 4, 1937, a simple metal folding chair became something. It became something that resulted in people buying more of them. The story behind the metal chair and how it changed people's behavior starts with a man named Sylvan Goldman. Goldman was a manager of a grocery store in Oklahoma City, Oklahoma. Goldman realized that if people could carry more, they would buy more.

Goldman went to Fred Young, a local handyman. He asked Young to make a shopping cart on wheels. Young attached wheels to the leg bottoms of a metal folding chair. Then he fitted two baskets to its front. The back of the chair acted as the cart's handle, and that's what people pushed. Goldman called the **altered** chair a "cartwheel."

Goldman took the altered folding chairs and then made something else. He knew that no one would use these strange contraptions at first. They wouldn't know what they were or how to use them. Goldman paid people to push their grocery-filled "cartwheels" around the store filled with groceries. Paying customers quickly took notice and began to push their own cartwheels. Sure enough, people bought more because they didn't have to worry about how full their hands were. They didn't have to worry about bulky or heavy items. It was just as easy to take two of something as one.

Check Your Understanding

1. What helps you to know that Goldman's strange contraption worked?
   a. Shopping carts are easy to push.
   b. Shopping carts are only used in grocery stores.
   c. Shopping carts are used in all kinds of stores today.
   d. Shopping carts have extra storage space under the basket.

2. What was the cartwheel's handle?
   a. the chair's legs
   b. the chair's back
   c. the chair's seat
   d. the chair's front

3. When something is **altered**, it is
   a. changed.
   b. strange.
   c. noticed.
   d. attached.

4. If you wanted to buy less, you would
   a. use a shopping cart.
   b. buy more than one of each item.
   c. only go shopping when you are hungry.
   d. only buy what you can carry.

/4

Name _____

Warm-Up

10   Undercover Zookeepers

The zookeepers at the San Diego Zoo went undercover. Dressed as tourists, they stood in front of a cage. Why were the zookeepers in disguise? Where were they standing?

The zookeepers stood in front of the orangutan enclosure. Orangutans are huge, orange apes. The zookeepers were secretly watching an orangutan named Ken Allen. Ken Allen was an escape artist. Zookeepers thought his cage was escape-proof, but Ken Allen had proved them wrong. So far, Ken Allen had escaped three times. He had unscrewed bolts, reached around to unlatch things, and climbed over walls. After each escape, Ken Allen would peacefully stroll around the zoo. He was never violent or aggressive. When zookeepers would come to lead him back to his cage, he

would follow them without objection. Ken Allen even helped other orangutans escape. It was as if he was having fun just trying to outwit his keepers.

Ken Allen had been **under surveillance** since he first escaped. But the zookeepers had to spy on him carefully. They tried dressing up as tourists. However, it wasn't until after they hired rock climbers that they could keep Ken Allen in his cage. The rock climbers found every finger-, toe-, and foothold within the enclosure. Then the zookeepers had to pay thousands of dollars to eliminate those areas!

Check Your Understanding

1. When you are **under surveillance**, you are
   a. escaping.
   b. in disguise.
   c. being closely watched.
   d. violent or aggressive.

2. *Eagle* is to *bird* as
   a. *orangutan* is to *ape*.
   b. *orangutan* is to *huge*.
   c. *orangutan* is to *orange*.
   d. *orangutan* is to *escape*.

3. From the context of the passage, you can infer that Ken Allen
   a. wanted to hurt people.
   b. wasn't very good at climbing.
   c. could recognize the zookeepers' uniforms.
   d. was unable to grasp things with his hands.

4. Most likely, if a visitor to the zoo saw an orangutan outside of its cage, he or she would
   a. climb into a cage.
   b. be very surprised.
   c. feel very peaceful.
   d. stroll peacefully by.

/4

Name _____

Fire Dogs

The Dalmatian is a breed of dog. It is known for its white coat with dark spots. In the United States, it is also known as a mascot for firefighters, or a firehouse dog. What is the origin of this relationship?

In the Middle Ages, Dalmatians were used as hunting dogs. In the 1800s, they were used as carriage dogs. They followed alongside horse-drawn coaches. Having been bred for stamina and energy, the dogs could easily keep up with the horses, even over long distances. It was the Dalmatians' loyalty, combined with its stamina and energy, that made it a superb carriage dog. Not only could the dog keep up, but it would also protect its owner's horses and carriage when the owner wasn't present.

Early firefighters used horse-drawn carriages. Oftentimes, the horses were fast and strong. This made the horses the choice of thieves. The Dalmatians would guard the horses at the firehouses. When there was a fire, the dogs would do what they had been trained to do. They would run in front of the horses and help clear a path. They made it so the firefighters could get to fires faster. As engines replaced horses, the dogs weren't needed in the same way. Instead, they became mascots. They were believed to bring firefighters good luck.

Check Your Understanding

1. All but what made the Dalmatian a superb fire dog?
   a. its energy
   b. its loyalty
   c. its ability to be trained
   d. its white coat with dark spots

2. All Dalmatian puppies are white. Most likely,
   a. their spots come in later.
   b. they are becoming a new breed.
   c. they are being bred to lose their spots.
   d. this keeps them safe from Dalmatian puppy thieves.

3. If you have the strength to carry on or endure, you have
   a. spots.
   b. stamina.
   c. loyalty.
   d. good luck.

4. Which of the following answers is written in the right order when it comes to how Dalmatians were used?
   a. mascots, hunting dogs, fire dogs
   b. hunting dogs, mascots, fire dogs
   c. hunting dogs, fire dogs, mascots
   d. fire dogs, hunting dogs, mascots

/4

Name _____

12 Gum in the Museum

Go to Washington, D.C. Enter the National Museum of American History. You will see a package of Wrigley's Juicy Fruit gum. You will see the receipt of its purchase, too. Nothing seems special about the gum. It is not the first gum made. It isn't even a new flavor. Why is it in the museum?

The gum's claim to fame came about on June 26, 1974. It was in a supermarket in Ohio. A customer pulled it out of his basket. He handed it to a clerk. The clerk scanned the package at 8:01 a.m. That's when the gum became the first item sold with a barcode using the Universal Product Code (UPC).

At first, people thought barcodes were not worth the time or money. This attitude soon changed. Grocers quickly saw the **benefits**

of the new technology. They could quickly identify fast-selling items. They could identify slow-selling items. By looking at historical data, grocers could tell when to order seasonal items.

Today, barcodes aren't limited to grocery stores. The technology has spread. For example, hospital patients are given bracelets with barcodes. Doctors and nurses can scan the bracelet. They can check a patient's identity. They can keep track of the patient's treatment and medicine.

Check Your Understanding

1. A grocer might want to identify a fast-selling item to
   a. change the UPC.
   b. send the item to other stores.
   c. quickly reorder the item to meet demand.
   d. put slow-moving items in better places.

2. Most likely, one reason the gum is in the museum is because
   a. the receipt shows the wrong UPC.
   b. it marks the first time gum was sold.
   c. a patient could not be in the museum.
   d. it marks the beginning use of a new technology.

3. Historical data is information
   a. taken from Ohio.
   b. taken over time.
   c. taken from hospitals.
   d. taken only in grocery stores.

4. When you see the **benefit** of something, you see the
   a. value.
   b. cost.
   c. risk.
   d. intelligence.

/4

Name _____

Athletes Wearing Plastic Bottles

In 2010, the World Cup Soccer tournament took place in South Africa. Many of the players wore plastic water bottles. To be exact, each athlete wore eight bottles. The bottles were taken from landfills. Why were players wearing garbage?

Landfills are beginning to fill up. Space for garbage is running out. To reduce waste, people can use less. They can also recycle. People are beginning to find new ways to recycle. One thing people have learned to do is reuse hard plastic. The plastic is melted down. It is made into other forms. Some of it is being spun into yarn. The yarn is then woven into a polyester fabric. The fabric is very soft.

Clothing companies are beginning to make clothes from this soft fabric. Some World Cup soccer teams wore jerseys made out of this fabric. The jerseys are very light. They are about 15 percent lighter than regular soccer jerseys. They also keep players cooler and drier by wicking, or drawing sweat away from the body.

The clothing company that made these shirts also made jerseys to sell. The company reported that it has used nearly thirteen million bottles from landfills. If these bottles were lined up end to end, they would stretch over 1,800 miles!

Check Your Understanding

1. From the context of the passage, you can infer that a jersey is a type of
a. shirt.
b. bottle.
c. plastic.
d. polyester.

2. Which of the following is *not* true about the jerseys made out of plastic?
a. They are cooler.
b. They are heavier.
c. They wick away sweat.
d. They are made out of eight bottles.

3. Which of the following facts is *not* that important to the passage?
a. Space for garbage is running out.
b. Hard plastic is being recycled into yarn.
c. The tournament took place in South Africa.
d. Some teams wore jerseys made out of plastic.

4. The passage is mainly about
a. four different kinds of fabric.
b. how many bottles are put in landfills.
c. what all World Cup soccer players wore.
d. clothing made from recycled hard plastic.

/4

Warm-Up

14

Name _____

Ludicrous Laws

When something is **ludicrous**, it is very silly. It is ridiculous. Some states and cities have silly laws on their books. The majority of these laws are outdated. They are not enforced. No one has bothered to go through the legal process to remove them.

Minnesota has a ludicrous law. The law says that you cannot cross over a state line if you are wearing a duck on your head. It makes you wonder if it is all right to wear a turkey on your head! In Missouri, it is illegal to drive a car with an uncaged bear. That law makes you wonder about what happened on the day it was decided the law was needed!

In Idaho, it is against the law for a man to give his sweetheart a box of candy weighing over fifty pounds. You have to wonder why it is legal for a man to give that same box of candy to a person who isn't his sweetheart!

Three other ludicrous laws are worth mentioning. In Georgia, it is against the law to keep a donkey in a bathtub. In Connecticut, it is against the law to walk across the street on your hands. In North Dakota, you can't go to bed with your shoes on.

Check Your Understanding

1. What state is correctly matched to the law mentioned in the passage?
   a. weight of candy box—Idaho
   b. walking on your hands—Missouri
   c. driving with a bear—Connecticut
   d. sleeping with shoes on—Minnesota

2. An antonym for **ludicrous** is
   a. funny.
   b. foolish.
   c. serious.
   d. ridiculous.

3. From the context of the passage, you can infer that
   a. all old laws are enforced.
   b. every state has the same laws.
   c. laws should always stay the same.
   d. different laws are needed over time.

4. What might someone say about the laws in the passage?
   a. They were for people who should be in jail.
   b. They were for people not using common sense.
   c. They were for people who were afraid of bears.
   d. They were for people who didn't like the legal process.

/4

Warm-Up

15

Name _____

If You Meet the Queen

The Queen of England is at home. How do you know she is in her palace? You take a look at the flagstaff on the building. If the Royal Standard (the queen's own personal flag) is flying, it means that the queen is at home. The Royal Standard can only be hoisted when the queen is in the building. The Royal Standard is a different flag from the English Union Jack flag.

You must stand when the queen enters a room. There is a "no-touch" rule when it comes to the queen, so you cannot hug or kiss her. If you shake the queen's hand, you cannot put out your hand first. You have to wait until the queen **extends** her hand, and then when you

do take it, you have to make sure you do not grip it tightly or pump it. You must address the queen as "Your Majesty," the first time you address her, but then you may simply address her as "Ma'am."

Americans do not have to curtsy or bow, as they are not subjects of the royal family, but still, it is polite for women to drop a small curtsy and for men to at least bow from the neck. You should not chew gum, and when the queen is finished eating, so are you.

Check Your Understanding

1. If someone calls the queen "Ma'am,"
   a. the person has to bow or curtsy.
   b. the person is not a subject of the royal family.
   c. it is the first time the person has addressed the queen.
   d. the person has already addressed the queen at least once.

2. From the context of the passage, you can infer that
   a. the Royal Standard is bigger than the Union Jack.
   b. the Union Jack is the flag of the British Empire.
   c. the Royal Standard is the flag of the British Empire.
   d. the Union Jack can only be flown when the queen is home.

3. If you are very hungry and you are going to dine with the queen, you might want to
   a. hug the queen before you sit down.
   b. ask for seconds after the queen is done.
   c. eat a bit first in case the queen isn't hungry.
   d. make sure you don't hold the silverware too tightly.

4. If something is **extended**, it is
   a. stretched out.
   b. gripped tightly.
   c. pumped up and down.
   d. brought close to the body.

/4

Name _____

A Snake for Healing

You have seen the staff of Aesculapius. It is used to represent the medical field. It is a rod with a serpent wrapped around it. Most people are afraid of serpents. They think of snakes as scary, slithery reptiles. Medicine is used to help. Doctors don't want their patients to be afraid of them. Why would the field of medicine have a symbol that uses an animal that many people are terrified of?

Despite how you feel about snakes, the serpent has long been a traditional symbol of healing. Long ago, Greeks felt that the snake had regenerative powers. (When something is *regenerated*, it is renewed. It is given new life.) Why did the Greeks feel a serpent had regenerative powers? Snakes occasionally shed their skin. As we grow, our skin grows. In contrast, a snake's skin does not grow. Snakes never stop growing, so a snake **periodically** has to shed its outer layer of skin and start fresh.

Aesculapius was the Roman god of medicine. His Greek name was Asclepius. The god may have been based on a skilled Greek doctor who practiced 2,000 years ago. Over time, myths and legends turned him into a god. In art, this god is sometimes represented as an old man holding a staff with a serpent wrapped around it.

Check Your Understanding

1. If a snake is very old,
   a. it is still growing.
   b. it is no longer growing.
   c. it stops being a reptile.
   d. it no longer sheds its skin.

2. When something happens **periodically**, it
   a. happens every day.
   b. happens only once.
   c. happens every ten years.
   d. happens once in a while.

3. What can regenerate?
   a. the leg of a giraffe
   b. the arm of a starfish
   c. the mouth of a monkey
   d. the head of an elephant

4. Snakes have come to represent the medical field, in part, because
   a. of people's fears.
   b. of their healing powers.
   c. of a traditional belief.
   d. of how they can wrap around a staff.

/4

Warm-Up

17

Name _____

Why Round?

Go to any city, and you will see manhole covers. Manholes are made so that workers can get to sewer lines, storm drains, or other subsurface utilities. Almost universally, every manhole cover is round. Why are manhole covers circular? Why aren't they rectangular? Why aren't they square?

Manhole covers are circular because that is the only shape that the cover cannot slip through. Rectangular or square covers can slip through the opening. All manhole covers rest on a lip. The lip is slightly smaller than the cover. The cover and the lip are manufactured together so the fit is close and tight.

Hold a rectangular cover on end. With the narrow side horizontal, and the long side vertical, the cover could be slipped into the hole. What if the cover was square? The diagonal of a square is longer than a side. When the cover is held on end, it can be slipped through the diagonal of the opening.

There is another advantage to a round cover. Manhole covers are heavy. An average cover weighs more than one hundred pounds. The heavy weight helps keep the cover in place. It also prevents **noxious** sewer gases from pushing up on the lid and popping it open. In addition, a round cover doesn't need to be lifted. It can be rolled.

Check Your Understanding

1. Most likely, a noxious gas
   a. can be rolled.
   b. only smells underground.
   c. smells bad or is harmful.
   d. only fits through a round hole.

2. Which of the following is *not* true about a square?
   a. It has four sides.
   b. It has straight sides.
   c. It has sides of equal length.
   d. It has a side longer than its diagonal.

3. The passage is mainly about
   a. shapes.
   b. manhole covers in one city.
   c. the weight of manhole covers.
   d. manhole covers around the world.

4. The word *subsurface* is used in the passage. Think of other words with "sub," like *submarine* or *submerge*. Most likely, the prefix "sub-" means
   a. on or above.
   b. after or later.
   c. below or under.
   d. start or begin.

/4

Warm-Up
18

Name _____

Who Is Calling?

You answer the telephone. The caller does not identify him or herself, but you know who it is. You recognize the voice. What if you couldn't recognize someone's voice?

There is a rare disorder called *phonagnosia*, commonly called "voice blindness." People with phonagnosia can tell if someone is male or female. They can tell if someone is mad or happy. They just can't identify who is speaking. One man who had it didn't know he had it until he was twenty-seven years old. When he was growing up, he could never understand how people knew it was him on the phone. It was a mystery. He finally decided that his voice must be very strange and sound very different from everyone else's.

The man learned to listen carefully when he answered the phone. He would use clues to identify the person. For example, he would know it was his mother if she talked about his brother.

The man was having a confusing time at work because his boss would call. Without identifying himself, his boss would fire off orders. The man's coworker noticed his confusion over several weeks. He finally asked why the man was confused. Didn't he recognize the boss's voice? That's when the man replied, "No! How could I?"

Check Your Understanding

1. Most likely, what most helps the man deal with his phonagnosia?
 a. texting
 b. ring tones
 c. caller ID
 d. volume control

2. What might be the most polite and helpful way to respond when someone picks up the phone?
 a. Tell them what you want.
 b. Ask them to speak clearly.
 c. greet and then identify yourself.
 d. make sure you have the correct number.

3. How old was the man when he discovered that he had phonagnosia?
 a. seventeen years old
 b. twenty-seven years old
 c. thirty-seven years old
 d. forty-seven years old

4. On the phone, a person with voice blindness cannot recognize
 a. a male voice.
 b. a speaker's voice.
 c. the sound of a happy voice.
 d. the sound of an angry voice.

/4

Warm-Up

19

Name _____

The Black Box

An airplane crashes. The search for the black box is on. What exactly is the black box? Why is it so important to flight-crash investigators? There are in fact two black boxes. The boxes are not black. They are bright orange and covered in a strip of reflective tape, as this makes them easier to find. They might be called black boxes because the first flight recorders were black. Others think it is because of how they look after being burned.

One black box is a flight data recorder (FDR). The other black box is a cockpit voice recorder (CVR). The FDR contains the last twenty-five hours of flight data. Flight data is tracked by sensors built into the airplane. Hundreds of parameters can be tracked, including acceleration, airspeed, altitude, flap settings, and engine performance. The CVR records two hours of sounds from the pilot's and copilot's headset. It also picks up sounds near the center of the cockpit.

Black boxes are made to survive all types of crashes. They can withstand fiery flames up to 2,000°F for one hour. They can survive deep saltwater and freshwater submersion up to thirty days. In addition, they send out a beacon for thirty days, even under the water.

Check Your Understanding

1. Which of the following types of data would be on the CVR?
   a. acceleration
   b. flap settings
   c. the pilot's words
   d. engine performance

2. Most likely, at the end of a tape, the black boxes
   a. stop recording.
   b. need to be replaced.
   c. erase all the old data.
   d. start to record over old data.

3. Black boxes can withstand fiery flames for at least
   a. one day.
   b. one hour.
   c. thirty days.
   d. thirty hours.

4. The passage is mainly about
   a. airplane flights.
   b. data-collecting tools.
   c. controls in the cockpit.
   d. flight-crash investigators.

/4

Warm-Up

20

Name _____

Memory Tricks

A mnemonic helps your memory. A mnemonic trick is like a shortcut for remembering information. You might be familiar with the mnemonic HOMES. HOMES is a mnemonic to help you remember the names of the Great Lakes. The names of the Great Lakes match the letters in the word **HOMES**. The Great Lakes are **H**uron, **O**ntario, **M**ichigan, **E**rie, and **S**uperior.

Mnemonics can be used in science. Think of the phrases "**K**ids **P**our **C**atsup **O**ver **F**at **G**reen **S**piders" and "**K**ing **P**hilip **C**ame **O**ver **F**or **G**ood **S**paghetti." The first letters of the words in these phrases stand for the divisions in the taxonomy classification system. The "k" is for kingdom. The "p" is for phylum.

The "c" is for class. The "o" is for order. The "f" is for family. The "g" is for genus. The "s" is for species.

See a rainbow, and the colors are always in the same order. The mnemonic **ROY G. BIV** can help you remember the order of the visible light spectrum. The order goes like this: red, orange, yellow, green, blue, indigo, violet. (Indigo is a deep violet-blue.) In a cave, you can see vertical mineral deposits called stalactites and stalagmites. You can use the mnemonic "Stala**c**tites are on the **c**eiling, and stala**g**mites are on the **g**round" to help you remember which one is which.

Check Your Understanding

1. The notes in the treble clef scale are *E, G, B, D, F*. What phrase might be a mnemonic for remembering the notes?
   a. Every Good Boy Does Fine
   b. Early Grapes Get Big Fast
   c. Every Giraffe Bites Down Hard
   d. Early Girls Build Better Forts

2. What order of colors can you find in the visible light spectrum?
   a. red, yellow, orange
   b. green, blue, indigo
   c. violet, orange, red
   d. yellow, violet, blue

3. "My Very Educated Mother Just Served Us Nuts" might be a mnemonic for the
   a. days of the week.
   b. names of the oceans.
   c. months of the year.
   d. order of the planets.

4. The American black bear is *Ursus americanus*. The polar bear is *Ursus maritimus*. The bears are in the same genus but *not* the same
   a. class.
   b. order.
   c. species.
   d. kingdom.

/4

Name _____

Warm-Up 21

The Nut That Must Be Shelled

You can buy hazelnuts and almonds shelled or unshelled. You can buy walnuts or pecans shelled or unshelled. There is only one nut that you have to buy shelled. You cannot buy it in the shell. The nut that you must buy shelled is the cashew.

The cashew nut is in a shell that looks like a really fat worm. The shell hangs from the underside of the cashew apple. The cashew apple is yellow or red. It looks somewhat like a pear or an oversized hot pepper. You can pluck off the cashew apple and eat it, so why can't you just crack open the shell and eat the cashew nut?

The cashew tree belongs to the same family as poison ivy. All members of this tree family produce an oily chemical that makes you burn and itch. With the cashew tree, the chemical is concentrated between two layers of the shell. To avoid being burned, you have to **extract** the nut very carefully. The process involves roasting, burning, boiling, soaking, cracking, and peeling. This explains why the old name for the cashew was the blister nut. It does not explain how a person ever decided that the nut was edible and worth eating in the first place!

Check Your Understanding

1. Which of the following items is edible?
   a. a pen
   b. a rug
   c. a book
   d. a carrot

2. The cashew was called the blister nut because its shell
   a. has seeds that look like oversized peppers.
   b. is shaped like a really fat blister.
   c. has a chemical that makes you burn and itch.
   d. hangs from the underside of the cashew apple.

3. A proverb is an old saying. What proverb fits the cashew nut?
   a. Practice makes perfect.
   b. You can't judge a book by its cover.
   c. A fool and his money are soon parted.
   d. An apple a day keeps the doctor away.

4. When you **extract** something, you
   a. pull it out.
   b. pluck it off.
   c. burn and itch.
   d. leave it unshelled.

/4

Warm-Up

22

Name _____

The Story Behind the Bug

In 1947, a computer at Harvard University wasn't working. Two men found the problem. The problem was a bug. It was a moth that had been trapped inside. The men removed the moth. They taped it to the computer log. Their entry read, "First actual case of bug being found." They also put out the word that they had "debugged" the machine. You can see the computer log with the moth in the Smithsonian Institution today.

Today, it is common to say that a computer has a bug. When a computer is fixed, it is common to say that it is debugged. These phrases became common after the moth was found. The truth is that the word "bug" was used before. It was used to describe an error or fault in any piece of machinery.

Thomas Edison was an inventor. One of Edison's inventions was the phonograph. A newspaper quoted Edison in 1889. Edison said that he "had been up the two previous nights searching for a bug in his phonograph." Unlike the bug in the Harvard computer, the bug in Edison's phonograph was just an error. It was not an error that also happened to be a real bug!

Check Your Understanding

1. What was Edison searching for in his phonograph?
   a. a meal
   b. a moth
   c. a machine
   d. a mistake

2. *Sofa* is to *couch* as
   a. *log* is to *cut*.
   b. *log* is to *water*.
   c. *log* is to *journal*.
   d. *log* is to *invention*.

3. Today, if someone says a computer has a bug, they most likely mean that
   a. a bug like a moth is trapped inside.
   b. the computer has something wrong with it.
   c. they have invented a new type of computer.
   d. they need to write an entry in a computer log.

4. Most likely, when the men made the entry in the computer log,
   a. they were having fun.
   b. they were really angry.
   c. they wanted to be quoted in a newspaper.
   d. they knew the log would be in the Smithsonian.

/4

Name _____

Setting Records

New Olympic records are being set all the time. Are people getting stronger? Are people today better athletes? People may be getting stronger, but athletes are also using better equipment.

For example, the first modern Olympic Games were in 1896. The record for the pole vault was ten feet, ten inches. The pole vaulter used a wooden pole. In 1940, the record pole vaulter did not use a wooden pole. He used a bamboo pole. Using the bamboo pole, the vaulter cleared fifteen feet. Bamboo poles are no longer used today. Fiberglass poles are. Fiberglass poles are springy. Using these new poles, vaulters can clear more than nineteen feet.

Equipment has also affected speed-skating times. Full body suits have helped skaters become more aerodynamic. This reduces drag. With the aerodynamic suits, skaters are able to push their way through the air with more ease. Clap skates were used in the 1998 Olympic Games. On traditional skates, the blade is fixed to the boot. On clap skates, the blade is attached to the boot by a hinge at the front. Clap skates allow a skater to use the leg's energy more efficiently. With clap skates, skaters went an average 4.3 miles per hour faster than before.

Check Your Understanding

1. Which of the following answers has the correct order of what types of poles that pole vaulters used, from old to new?
   a. wood, fiberglass, bamboo
   b. bamboo, wood, fiberglass
   c. wood, bamboo, fiberglass
   d. fiberglass, bamboo, wood

2. Newly designed oars were used in the 1996 Olympic Games. This fact would explain why the athletes in the 1996 Olympic Games had
   a. faster times than the athletes in the 1992 Olympic Games.
   b. slower times than the athletes in the 1992 Olympic Games.
   c. faster times than the athletes in the 2000 Olympic Games.
   d. slower times than the athletes in the 2000 Olympic Games.

3. If a weaker athlete has a better time than a stronger athlete, it may be because
   a. the same equipment was used.
   b. different equipment was used.
   c. the athletes were both skaters.
   d. the athletes were both swimmers.

4. Swimmers today are beating older records all the time. This may be because
   a. new pools are being built.
   b. swimmers are allowed to cheat.
   c. past swimmers were more efficient.
   d. more aerodynamic suits are being worn.

/4

Name _____

Duct Tape

Duct tape was first made in the early 1940s. Its original use was to keep moisture out of ammunition cases. People began to call the tape "duck tape." Just like a duck's feathers, it was waterproof. Also, it was made using cotton duck. Cotton duck is a heavy, plain cotton fabric.

People soon found that the tape was **versatile**. Not only could it be used for cases, but it could also be used for other household items. The name changed to "duct tape" when house builders began using the tape to connect heating and cooling ducts together. (A *duct* is a tube or channel through which a gas or liquid moves.) The original color of duct tape was army green. Then it was changed to silver, a common color of house ducts. Today, it is sold in a variety of colors.

Two examples demonstrate the tape's versatility. First, *Apollo 13* astronauts used it to save their lives. They modified parts to make a temporary lifeboat. Second, a man came to a doctor with a painful rash after a surprise meeting with a tarantula. Feeling threatened, the tarantula had defended itself by rubbing its back legs against its abdomen. This had caused thousands of tiny barbed hairs to shoot out. The duct tape was used to remove the barbed hairs causing the rash!

Check Your Understanding

1. The passage is mainly about
   a. astronauts on *Apollo 13*.
   b. how tarantulas defend themselves.
   c. where the name "duct tape" came from.
   d. duct tape and some ways it is used.

2. Which of the following could be the correct order of colors in which duct tape was made?
   a. silver, red, green
   b. green, silver, blue
   c. green, black, silver
   d. orange, green, silver

3. The passage does *not* tell you
   a. how duct tape is used.
   b. who invented duct tape.
   c. if duct tape is waterproof.
   d. what the first duct tape was made from.

4. If something is **versatile**,
   a. it can only be one color.
   b. it can be any color but green.
   c. it can be used for only one thing.
   d. it can be used for many different things.

/4

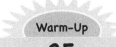

Warm-Up

25

Name _____

What the Appraisers Knew

An appraiser decides what things are worth. For example, an appraiser may appraise antiques or works of art. An appraiser has to be able to judge if something is well made. An appraiser also has to know what other similar items have sold for.

An appraiser is shown a five-dollar bill from the United States. The bill looks and feels old. Like all of the five-dollar bills printed today, it has a picture of Abraham Lincoln on it. Abraham Lincoln was the sixteenth president of the United States. The bill is dated 1845. The appraiser takes one look at the bill. He says, "This bill is worthless. It is a forgery."

An appraiser is shown a painting. The painting looks as if it is very old. It is an oil painting of a scene from South America. It is

a picture of an Incan couple from Peru. The man is leading a llama, and the woman is holding a chicken. The painting is dated 1450. The appraiser takes one look at the painting. She says, "This painting is worthless. It is a forgery."

How did the appraisers know? Lincoln was president from 1861 to 1865. His picture would not have been on a bill from 1845. Chickens weren't brought to the Americas until the 1500s. They were introduced by Spanish explorers.

Check Your Understanding

1. From the context of the passage, you can infer that, for some items, appraisers must know their
   a. math facts.
   b. science facts.
   c. English facts.
   d. history facts.

2. Most likely, what animal is native to South America?
   a. the cow
   b. the horse
   c. the llama
   d. the chicken

3. If an appraiser is appraising a house, he or she might want to know
   a. what newer houses in the area sold for.
   b. what bigger houses in the area sold for.
   c. what smaller houses in the area sold for.
   d. what similar houses in the area sold for.

4. Lincoln was president during the Civil War. The war could have happened in what years?
   a. 1500–1504
   b. 1845–1849
   c. 1861–1865
   d. 1932–1936

/4

Warm-Up

26

Name _____

Seen from the Moon

An artifact is a thing or object. It is made by human work or skill. Ask a person what man-made objects can be seen from the moon with the naked eye. Most people will answer that there is only one thing. They will answer that it is the Great Wall of China. This answer is incorrect. The truth is that no man-made artifacts can be seen from the moon with the naked eye. Why are so many people wrong?

People are confused. They are confusing the moon with space. Space is quite close. It begins where Earth's atmosphere ends. There is no pinpoint location, but space starts at about sixty-two miles above the planet's surface. The National Aeronautics and Space Administration is known as NASA. NASA calls anyone who flies higher than fifty miles outside of the atmosphere an astronaut.

Many man-made artifacts on Earth can be seen from space. One object is indeed the Great Wall of China. Other artifacts include motorways, cities, and fields of crops. Even some individual buildings can be pointed out. A few thousand miles into deep space, though, no man-made artifacts are visible. The moon is more than 250,000 miles away. At that distance, it is impossible to see any man-made artifacts. At that distance, even the continents are barely visible.

Check Your Understanding

1. Who would NASA call an astronaut?
   a. a person who flies five miles up
   b. a person who flies twenty-five miles up
   c. a person who flies forty-five miles up
   d. a person who flies sixty-five miles up

2. Which of the following objects is not an artifact?
   a. a stone
   b. a stone axe
   c. a stone wall
   d. a stone pathway

3. From the context of the passage, which of the following statements is true?
   a. You can see cities from the moon.
   b. You can see the continents from the moon.
   c. You can see fields of crops from the moon.
   d. You can see the Great Wall of China from the moon.

4. Another title for the passage might be
   a. "Common Mistakes."
   b. "Where Space Begins."
   c. "What's Visible from Far Away."
   d. "Why People Are Confused About Astronauts."

/4

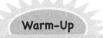

Warm-Up

27

Name _____

The First Coin with Braille

The United States Mint issued fifty state quarters. Each state had a different design. The quarters were released over ten years. They were issued in the order the states ratified the Constitution or were admitted to the Union. Each quarter was produced for ten weeks only and will not be minted ever again.

Did you know that one of the quarters was the first U.S. coin with Braille? Braille is a method of reading that allows blind people to read. The Braille system is set up with cells and uses raised dots. Each cell is made up of two columns with three dots each. Dots can be raised at any of the six positions in the cell. Different combinations of raised dots stand for different letters of the alphabet.

What quarter has Braille on it? The Alabama state quarter has the name Helen Keller written out in raised dots. Alabama was the 22nd state admitted to the Union, so it was the 22nd quarter to be released. It was released in 2003. On the quarter, Keller is seated and reading a book in Braille. Despite becoming blind and deaf at a young age, Keller learned to read and write. She spoke by using her hands to sign. She listened by feeling other people's signs.

Check Your Understanding

1. What sense is needed for the Braille system to work?
   a. smell
   b. sight
   c. touch
   d. hearing

2. Which of the following answers is *not* true about the Braille system?
   a. It uses raised dots.
   b. It is made up of cells and raised dots.
   c. Each cell has two columns.
   d. Each column has four dots.

3. The passage is mainly about
   a. a coin.
   b. fifty states.
   c. famous people.
   d. the Constitution.

4. Texas was the 28th state admitted to the Union. This means that the Texas state quarter was released
   a. in 2002.
   b. after the Alabama state quarter.
   c. before the Alabama state quarter.
   d. at the same time as the Alabama state quarter.

/4

Name _____

Do You Know Chameleons?

Do you know what chameleons do? Many people think that these special lizards change color to match their backgrounds. They think the chameleons change color to camouflage themselves. This is not true at all. Chameleons can change color, but it is not to match their backgrounds. It is not for camouflage.

A chameleon's skin has several layers of specialized cells. The cells are called chromatophores, and they contain differently colored pigments. These cells lie in layers under the chameleon's outer, transparent skin. Certain things can cause the balance between these cells to change. Some cells can become enlarged, while others can shrink. A chameleon's skin color depends on the balance between the cells.

What affects the balance between the cell layers? It is not the chameleon's background. It is the chameleon's mood. A chameleon may change color if it is scared. It may change color if it beats another chameleon in a fight. It may change color if it sees a chameleon of the opposite sex. It may change color if it gets too hot or cold.

If this is news to you, don't feel you are the only one who was misinformed. This myth can be traced back to 240 BCE! It was included in the stories of Antigonus of Carystus, an ancient Greek writer.

Check Your Understanding

1. A chameleon will *not* change color
   a. if it gets scared.
   b. if it wins a fight.
   c. if its background changes.
   d. if it gets too hot or cold.

2. From the context of the passage, what can you infer about myths?
   a. Some myths are passed down for centuries.
   b. The first myth was written in 240 BCE.
   c. There is never any truth to Greek myths.
   d. There are more myths about chameleons than other lizards.

3. The passage is mainly about
   a. lizards.
   b. chameleons' skin.
   c. specialized cells.
   d. ancient Greek myths.

4. *Enlarge* is to *shrink* as
   a. *change* is to *alter*.
   b. *misinform* is to *lie*.
   c. *scare* is to *frighten*.
   d. *camouflage* is to *display*.

/4

Warm-Up

29

Name _____

Uluru

Sometimes when you see an interesting rock, you pick it up and put it in your pocket. Some interesting rocks are collected and put into museums. There is one rock that you will never pick up. You will never put it in your pocket. You will never see it in a museum. This is because the rock is colossal. It is gigantic. It is **enormous**. It is the largest rock in the world.

This mammoth rock is in the center of Australia. It stands by itself in the semi-arid landscape where only about twelve inches of rain falls a year. The rock was named by the original inhabitants of Australia. It is called Uluru. Made of red sandstone, the rock stands 1,142 feet high. Its circumference, or distance around, is about 5.8 miles. If you wanted to walk around it, it would take several hours.

Uluru is ancient. It dates back over 500 million years. It is all that is left of an **eroded** mountain range. Many people are unaware that they are not even seeing half of the rock. Most of the rock is underground. Uluru is famous for changing colors as different light strikes it at different times of the day and year.

Check Your Understanding

1. Which of the following words is *not* a synonym for **enormous**?
   a. mammoth
   b. ancient
   c. colossal
   d. gigantic

2. How much of Uluru is underground?
   a. none
   b. exactly 1/2
   c. more than 1/2
   d. less than 1/2

3. When something is **eroded**, it is
   a. worn away.
   b. semi-arid.
   c. underground.
   d. interesting.

4. The passage is mainly about
   a. collecting rocks.
   b. what Uluru is made of.
   c. what Uluru is famous for.
   d. the largest rock in the world.

/4

Warm-Up

30   The Mummy's Passport

Name _____

When people visit another country, they need passports. Each country has its own passport. A passport identifies who someone is. It is like an international identification badge. Passports are stamped when people enter and exit countries.

Did you know that there is a mummy who was issued a passport? The mummy was in Egypt. He needed to go to France. When the mummy got there, his passport was stamped. He was also met in a special way. He was met with full military honors. Why would a mummy go to France? Why would a mummy be received with military honors?

The mummy was an Egyptian pharaoh. His name was Ramesses II. Ramesses reigned from 1279–13 BCE. When he died, he was mummified and laid in a tomb. Today, his mummy rests in Cairo's Egyptian Museum. In 1974, people saw that the mummy was rotting. They needed to fly the ancient king to France for help.

Ramesses was issued a passport so he could enter the country. How was Ramesses' occupation listed? It was listed as "King (**deceased**)." As befitting any royal visitor, Ramesses was met with military honors. Then he was diagnosed with a fungal infection. After treatment, Ramesses was flown back to Egypt.

Check Your Understanding

1. When something is **deceased**, it is
   a. dead.
   b. alive.
   c. stamped.
   d. infected.

2. Which of the following sentences best sums up the passage?
   a. It is about the reign of Ramesses and Egypt.
   b. It is about passports and how mummies are made.
   c. It is about passports and an ancient king who needed one.
   d. It is about a French king who was met with military honors.

3. *Occupation* is to *king* as
   a. *job* is to *tomb*.
   b. *job* is to *pharaoh*.
   c. *job* is to *passport*.
   d. *job* is to *France*.

4. Which of the following information is, most likely, *not* found on a passport?
   a. your name
   b. your eye color
   c. your date of birth
   d. your favorite food

/4

Fascinating People

Warm-Up 1

Name _____

Running Around the World

Robert Garside was irritating his cell mates. What was Garside doing to bother the other prisoners? He was running in place nonstop so that he could stay in shape. Garside was on a quest to run around the world. To complete his quest, Garside had to run from place to place. He could not walk or use any other means of transportation. He was only allowed to fly when he was going from one land mass to another.

Garside ran for over five years. He traveled across twenty-nine countries and went through fifty pairs of running shoes. Garside had many adventures. He was imprisoned in one country because he did not have proper papers. Fortunately, after irritating his cellmates for several days with his running in place, he was allowed to run to the border and out of the country.

Some people say that while Garside ran for thousands of miles, he did not actually run the distance he said he did. They say Garside's claim is a hoax, or trick. They say Garside was not always where he said he was. People often ran with Garside, but other times Garside was by himself. No one will ever know exactly how many miles Garside ran. What is known for sure is that running around the world is not easy. It is an extraordinarily difficult feat.

Check Your Understanding

1. Why might it have been hard for Garside to prove he was in the places he said he was?
   a. He had to spend time in prison.
   b. He needed papers to cross borders.
   c. There were not always people where he ran.
   d. He was using different means of transportation.

2. The main idea of the passage is
   a. one man's quest.
   b. staying in shape.
   c. getting out of prison.
   d. traveling from land mass to land mass.

3. The passage does *not* tell you
   a. why Garside was imprisoned.
   b. where Garside was imprisoned.
   c. what Garside did when he was imprisoned.
   d. who Garside irritated when he was imprisoned.

4. Something done that shows great courage, skill, or strength is a
   a. cell.
   b. hoax.
   c. feat.
   d. trick.

/4

Warm-Up

2

Name _____

Nurse on Board

Air travel was still a new form of transportation in the 1920s. Most people preferred a train because they felt flying was too dangerous. If airlines wanted more passengers, they had to convince the public that flying was safe. What could the airlines do to convince the public?

Ellen Church came up with the solution. Church was born on September 22, 1904. She was a nurse. Church fell in love with flying, and she took pilot lessons. She wanted to be hired as a pilot, but she was told she could not be one because she was a woman. Then she said that she should be hired as a flight attendant. She said that having nurses on board would help people feel they were safe.

Church became the first flight attendant on May 15, 1930. The publicity and reaction to Church was so great that the airlines decided to make flight attendants the norm. The first flight attendants were required to be nurses. They had to be single and younger than twenty-five. They could not be over five feet, four inches tall or weigh more than 115 pounds. They had to take care of passengers, but they also had to haul luggage and fuel planes. At times, they even had to help pilots push planes into hangars!

Check Your Understanding

1. The passage is mainly about
   a. transportation.
   b. making planes safer.
   c. the first flight attendant.
   d. who could take pilot lessons.

2. From the context of the passage, you can infer that when Church was hired,
   a. she was not married.
   b. she was not a nurse.
   c. she was not afraid of trains.
   d. she was not liked by the public.

3. *Plane* is to *hangar* as
   a. *kite* is to *tail*.
   b. *car* is to *garage*.
   c. *rocket* is to *moon*.
   d. *boat* is to *captain*.

4. Airlines made flight attendants the norm because
   a. nurses could not be pilots.
   b. people felt safe on board trains.
   c. the public fell in love with flying.
   d. the reaction to Church's solution was so great.

/4

Warm-Up

3

Name _____

Fire!

"Everyone inside. Now!" No one wanted to obey Ed Pulaski, but he had a gun. Pulaski was a U.S. Forest Service Ranger in Idaho. The day was August 20, 1910. All around them, one of the biggest forest fires in the history of the United States was raging.

Pulaski knew his men's instinct was to run, but there was nowhere to go. They didn't want to enter the dark, abandoned mine he was insisting they go into. Its door timbers were on fire, and the men could feel the oxygen being sucked out by the raging fire outside. Yet Pulaski knew that if any of them were to survive, they would have to remain in the mine. The trail they had trod just moments before was already covered in flames.

Pulaski forced his men face down onto the ground where there was more oxygen. Pulaski stayed by the door and fought the fire with blankets and his bare hands. One by one, the men passed out from lack of oxygen. Five hours later, the men began to come to. They saw Pulaski unconscious by the door and thought he was dead. Then Pulaski rose up. Only able to see out of one eye, and with his face, hands, and body badly burned, Pulaski led his men through the still smoldering forest to safety.

Check Your Understanding

1. Pulaski's actions could best be called
   a. cruel.
   b. heroic.
   c. useless.
   d. cowardly.

2. The author wrote this article to
   a. demonstrate how to fight fires.
   b. show how important oxygen is.
   c. provide a history of forest fires.
   d. share a story about a forest ranger.

3. What day did Pulaski force his men into the mine?
   a. July 20, 1910
   b. July 10, 1920
   c. August 20, 1910
   d. August 10, 1920

4. You are escaping from a smoky room. Most likely, you should
   a. stand up straight and run out.
   b. run even if there is nowhere to go.
   c. be ready to fight the fire with your bare hands.
   d. crawl because there is more oxygen close to the ground.

/4

Name _____

Why a New Grove

Margaret D. Lowman is a biologist who studies tree canopies. Tree canopies are formed by plant crowns and are the above-ground portion of a plant community. To get to a tree canopy, Lowman would use a special slingshot to shoot a rope over a branch. Then she would climb high up into the leafy canopy.

One time, Lowman was in Australia. She found a grove of trees in the rainforest that no one had ever studied before. She set traps to study leaf litter and picked out the trees she would climb. After a month, she went back to her secret grove to look in the traps and climb trees. As she neared the grove, she felt the ground near her feet moving. Lowman had just missed stepping on an Australian brown snake! These vipers are very aggressive and extremely poisonous. As Lowman began to look around, she saw more and more of the vipers. The ground was crawling with poisonous snakes! They had all come to bask in the sun.

Slowly and carefully, Lowman made her way out of the grove and back to her car. When she was safe, she knew it was time to look for a new grove of trees. She needed a grove where she could concentrate on trees and not on what was slithering beneath them!

Check Your Understanding

1. The passage is mainly about
   a. tree canopies.
   b. what biologists do.
   c. the Australian brown snake.
   d. why one grove wasn't studied.

2. What could *not* be part of the tree canopy?
   a. moss
   b. roots
   c. leaves
   d. branches

3. Most likely, Lowman first saw the grove
   a. at a time when it wasn't so hot.
   b. after other people had found it.
   c. before the trees had gotten so tall.
   d. when the trees didn't have any leaves.

4. If you called someone a "viper," most likely, the person was
   a. tall and green.
   b. sweet and liked to sing.
   c. mean and could not be trusted.
   d. very small and could not swim.

/4

Warm-Up

5

Name _____

A Mystery Solved

Percival Lowell was an astronomer. He was a good observer who was hardworking and honest. He knew a lot about math and even helped advance the field of astronomy. The name for the dwarf planet Pluto was, in part, chosen for his initials "P" and "L." Yet Lowell always said there was a dark spot on Venus. He said there was a pattern on the planet, too. The pattern was made of spindly spokes. Lowell insisted he was right. Other astronomers did not agree with Lowell. They said what he was seeing was not real; it was an illusion.

Today, we know that Lowell was wrong about Venus. It has been a mystery how Lowell could be so right about so many things and so wrong about Venus. Lowell was born in 1855, and he drew his map of Venus in 1896. It is only now that people think the mystery has been solved.

When Lowell made his observations, he found that he could see Venus's spokes best when his telescope was at a particular setting. This setting often casts shadows of blood vessels on the eye's retina, making them visible. Lowell was not mapping spoke-like structures on the surface of Venus. He was mapping the blood vessels in his own eyes!

Check Your Understanding

1. Who might have helped to solve the mystery?
   a. a surgeon
   b. an eye doctor
   c. a heart doctor
   d. a kidney doctor

2. Most likely, the dark spot Lowell said he saw
   a. was also something in his retina.
   b. was discovered to be a dwarf planet.
   c. was a speck of dirt on his telescope.
   d. was seen by astronomers with better telescopes.

3. When you think something is real but it is *not*, it is
   a. a spoke.
   b. a pattern.
   c. an illusion.
   d. a structure.

4. Which of the following answers is *not* true?
   a. Lowell was hardworking.
   b. Lowell was born in 1896.
   c. Lowell was an astronomer.
   d. Lowell was a good observer.

/4

Name _____

Warm-Up
6

Shark Lady

The captain couldn't believe his eyes. His passenger Eugenie Clark was going to get into shark-infested waters! The captain warned his passenger, but she told him that was exactly why she was going into the water.

Eugenie Clark was a marine biologist. She studied sharks, and she needed to collect some living specimens. She wanted to conduct some experiments on sharks to measure their intelligence. Were they just vicious eating machines always ready to attack, or could they learn?

The captain warned Clark that there might be more sharks than usual in the water. This was because they had set baited hooks. If a shark had been hooked and had started to bleed, it would attract even more sharks. Holding up

a pressurized can, Clark told the captain she was ready. All she had to do was spray the contents of the can down the shark's throat, and it would knock it unconscious. An unconscious shark would be easier to bring in.

By the end of the day, Clark had caught a lemon shark. It was a specimen worth taking back to the lab. Later, Clark did experiments on lemon sharks. She showed that they were more than vicious eating machines. They were intelligent. They could learn to hit a board, which would ring a bell and alert someone to get them food.

Check Your Understanding

1. What type of specimen did Clark collect?
   a. a blue shark
   b. a reef shark
   c. a lemon shark
   d. a tiger shark

2. Which of the following adjectives doesn't fit Clark?
   a. brave
   b. daring
   c. curious
   d. vicious

3. *Awake* is to *asleep* as
   a. *eat* is to *food.*
   b. *bell* is to *ring.*
   c. *intelligent* is to *smart.*
   d. *conscious* is to *unconscious.*

4. The passage is mainly about
   a. a marine biologist.
   b. what a sea captain said.
   c. an experiment with a bell.
   d. how intelligent sharks are.

/4

Name _____

Just Water

James Herriot was a veterinarian (vet, for short). One time, a farmer called him to his house. The farmer raised cattle, and he was very worried about his bull. The bull was expensive, and it would be hard and costly to replace. The farmer was afraid the bull was going to die because it was so ill. He thought that if treatment were possible, he would not be able to afford it.

Herriot took a look at the bull. It was having difficulty breathing. It gasped for air as its mighty rib cage laboriously rose and fell. Its mouth gaped open, and bubbling foam hung around its lips. Herriot took its temperature. It was a whopping 110°F.

Herriot had never seen such a high temperature before, but when he measured it again, the temperature was just as high.

Herriot was clueless. Strange diseases and their symptoms ran through his mind as he worried that the bull would die. Then he happened to glance at the sun. Suddenly he asked, "Has the bull been out today?" When the answer was **affirmative**, Herriot told the farmer to rush and get a hose. The bull didn't have a strange disease requiring expensive medicine or costly treatment. All it needed was to be drenched in cold water because it was suffering from sunstroke!

Check Your Understanding

1. When an answer is in the **affirmative**,
   a. it means "no."
   b. it means "yes."
   c. it means "maybe."
   d. it means that it is unknown.

2. What gave Herriot the final clue he needed?
   a. seeing the sun
   b. the bull's labored breathing
   c. taking the bull's temperature
   d. the foam around the bull's lips

3. Another title for the passage might be
   a. "A Vet's Tale."
   b. "Raising Cattle."
   c. "Expensive Medicine."
   d. "How Water Stops Diseases."

4. How would Herriot know he had been right?
   a. The bull would die.
   b. The farmer would pay.
   c. The bull would suffer.
   d. The bull's symptoms would stop.

/4

Name _____

A Sticky Lesson

Karen DeSanto was excited. For the first time, she was going to be paid for being a clown. It was a summer evening. The hot sun was just beginning to set. DeSanto was performing outside at a children's birthday party. Standing under the porch lights, she started her tricks. Unfortunately, the children weren't laughing. They were bored. Some looked like they were going to fall asleep.

DeSanto had covered her face in greasepaint. The greasepaint was white and sticky. Much to DeSanto's dismay, a giant gnat landed on her face. Trapped by the **tacky** greasepaint, the gnat fluttered wildly against DeSanto's cheek. DeSanto continued with her tricks, but her troubles only got worse as more and more gnats began to get stuck on her face. Soon,

her face was covered with wildly beating insects. DeSanto's young audience may have been disgusted, but they were wide awake!

DeSanto learned that to apply the greasepaint properly, you should powder it. The powder makes it less sticky. DeSanto learned even more after she was accepted into Clown College. DeSanto had to compete against thousands of other clowns to get into Clown College. After graduating, DeSanto went on to work as a circus clown. She also worked as a clown instructor, teaching other clowns how to perfect their acts.

Check Your Understanding

1. All but what led to the gnats getting stuck on DeSanto's face?
a. DeSanto was outside.
b. The hot sun was just beginning to set.
c. DeSanto put powder on her greasepaint.
d. DeSanto was standing under porch lights.

2. *Gnat* is to *insect* as
a. *cat* is to *mammal*.
b. *fish* is to *trout*.
c. *flower* is to *daisy*.
d. *reptile* is to *snake*.

3. Someone who wants to be a clown might want to find out more about
a. gnats.
b. Clown College.
c. sleeping tricks.
d. staying wide awake.

4. When something is **tacky**, it is
a. hot.
b. white.
c. greasy.
d. sticky.

/4

Warm-Up

9

Name _____

A Fast Descent

Finally, Ernest Shackleton and his men made it to the top of the ridge. The ridge was so sharp that they could sit astride it, one leg on either side. Shackleton and his men were at the top, but they were in extreme danger. They had barely any food, zero camping equipment, and their clothes were ragged tatters. It was well after four o'clock, and a thick, blinding fog was creeping up behind them. Soon, they would be unable to see. If they did not make a speedy descent, they would freeze to death.

Shackleton and his men were trying to cross South Georgia Island. This icy island was unmapped and had never been crossed before. Shackleton and his men had been shipwrecked, and they were seeking help at a whaling station. It had taken them hours of struggle to get to the top of the snowy ridge. Weak, hungry, and cold, they thought the end had finally come.

Then Shackleton said, "We're going to slide." His men could not believe it, but Shackleton knew there was no **alternative**. With Shackleton in front, the men sat on their rope, grabbed onto each other, and pushed off. They slid so fast that they could not breathe. Yet, miraculously, they survived. In less than two minutes, they descended over 2,000 feet.

Check Your Understanding

1. If you have no other **alternative**, you
   a. are sitting astride.
   b. have no other choice.
   c. are making a fast descent.
   d. miraculously survive.

2. Which of the following best describes Shackleton?
   a. Shackleton didn't ever use maps.
   b. Shackleton didn't give up easily.
   c. Shackleton didn't have imagination.
   d. Shackleton didn't care about his men.

3. We know about Shackleton's slide because
   a. he was shipwrecked.
   b. the island was icy.
   c. he reached the whaling station.
   d. his clothes were ragged tatters.

4. The author's main purpose was to
   a. tell you about a great leader.
   b. tell you how to climb a ridge.
   c. tell you about a whaling station.
   d. tell you about being shipwrecked.

/4

Name _____

A River Test

Brigit Crocker was on a raft. A river guide, Crocker was leading a white river-rafting expedition in the Philippines. She was in a remote and wild area when something splashed down in the water next to her. It had been thrown by some people who were standing on a swinging rope bridge above the river. The people on the bridge were known for their fierceness, and they didn't look friendly as they silently stared down at Crocker.

Crocker wanted to keep her passengers safe, so she knew she couldn't make the people above her angry. Reaching with her paddle, she pulled what had been thrown into the water onto her watercraft. It was a dead and rotting piglet. Crocker didn't want it, but thinking it was a gift, she held it up and smiled her thanks. The people above Crocker only looked angry.

Then with a shout, Crocker's Philippine guides told her to throw the piglet back in the water. The piglet wasn't a gift; it was a test! No sane and intelligent person would want a rotting piglet. It wasn't until Crocker threw the piglet back into the water that the people on the bridge began to cheer and whistle. Crocker had proved that she was intelligent and that her mind was **sound**.

Check Your Understanding

1. Most likely, Crocker had been told before that
a. not accepting gifts was rude.
b. you should never accept gifts.
c. it was okay to make people angry.
d. she wouldn't need a Philippine guide.

2. The word *sound* has more than one meaning. In the passage, the word **sound** means
a. normal and healthy.
b. deep and secretive.
c. to make known or announce.
d. noise, anything that can be heard.

3. From the context of the passage, you can infer that
a. you never need more than one guide.
b. guides mostly work on river expeditions.
c. in the Philippines, you don't need a guide.
d. part of a guide's job is passenger safety.

4. What fact from the passage helps you to understand how wild and remote the area was?
a. People stood on the bridge.
b. The bridge was made of rope.
c. The bridge went across the river.
d. Something was tossed from the bridge.

/4

Warm-Up

11

Name _____

What to Say

Chuck Yeager is the man who broke the sound barrier. People were afraid that if you traveled faster than sound, something bad might happen. The plane and the pilot might be greatly harmed. On October 14, 1947, Yeager flew at a speed faster than sound. This story though is not about that **inaugural** flight. It is about a flight Yeager took in January 1946.

Yeager was in a two-seat T-6 prop trainer running a power-speed test. A master rod blew apart in the engine, and Yeager had to make an emergency landing. Yeager was over Ohio farmland, and with the plane vibrating wildly, he set himself down between two fields.

He hit the ground with the wheels up and crashed through a chicken house. Boards clattered and feathers flew. The plane continued to slide, and its right wing hit a smokehouse. This caused the plane to turn, and the plane's tail hit the front end of a porch. This, in turn, made the plane turn some more, and it came to rest directly outside the kitchen of the farmhouse.

The farmer's wife was at the kitchen sink. Yeager was able to look her directly in the eye. What do you say in a situation like this? Yeager raised the plane's canopy. He smiled and said, "Morning, Ma'am. Can I use your telephone?"

Check Your Understanding

1. Most likely, the farmer's wife was
   a. expecting Yeager.
   b. shocked by Yeager.
   c. pleased to meet Yeager.
   d. happy that Yeager broke the sound barrier.

2. Yeager broke the sound barrier
   a. about 1 ¾ years after his emergency landing.
   b. about 2 ¾ years after his emergency landing.
   c. about 1 ¾ years before his emergency landing.
   d. about 2 ¾ years before his emergency landing.

3. From the context of the passage, you can infer that perhaps Yeager was chosen to break the sound barrier because
   a. he had to pay back the farmer.
   b. he waited to be told what to do.
   c. he stayed calm in emergency situations.
   d. he called his base no matter where he landed.

4. Yeager's breaking the sound barrier was an *inaugural* flight. Most likely, **inaugural** means
   a. to crash or hit.
   b. to land or crash.
   c. to end or finish.
   d. to begin or start.

/4

Name _____

The Windsock That Dangled

Beryl Markham was flying in darkness over the lonely and wild Kenyan landscape. Markham was born in 1902. She became a pilot when flying was still new and a very unusual profession for a woman. She was in a small plane by herself, and she was delivering medical supplies. Markham could just make out her makeshift landing strip. It was tiny, dirty, and outlined by a few crude oil torches.

Markham circled the field before landing. She looked at the direction of the torch flames, trying to gauge the wind direction. Due to her skill, she was able to land safely. After the medical supplies were unloaded, a man told her how they had prepared the landing strip for her. "We even rigged up a windsock," he told her. Despite the wind, the windsock at the end of the pole just **dangled** limply. Markham walked over and discovered why. Instead of its end being open so the wind could flow through, its end had been stitched together, like the toe of a sock.

Over the years, Markham did more than deliver medical supplies to remote places. She was the first woman to fly **solo** and nonstop across the Atlantic from east to west. She left England on September 4, 1936, and touched ground again in Nova Scotia. Her entire trip took twenty hours.

Check Your Understanding

1. From the context of the passage, you can infer that a windsock should
   a. have two open ends.
   b. have flames like a torch.
   c. be stitched at both ends.
   d. have a closed end like a sock.

2. When you fly **solo**, you fly
   a. alone.
   b. at night.
   c. east to west.
   d. with the wind.

3. The passage is mainly about
   a. a flight from England.
   b. how a man made a windsock.
   c. delivering medical supplies.
   d. a woman who was a pioneer pilot.

4. What person is **dangling**?
   a. the one cutting a tree branch
   b. the one sitting on a tree branch
   c. the one climbing on a tree branch
   d. the one hanging from a tree branch

/4

Warm-Up 13

Name _____

Only Faster

Twelve miles of straight lines were marked out in the Black Rock Desert in Nevada. The car that would race on this track would only be timed for one mile. Why were so many more miles marked out? The car needed distance to reach maximum speed, and it needed six miles to stop. Just how fast was this car going to go?

The car was the Thrust SSC (SuperSonic Car). It was driven by Andy Green, an English Royal Air Force pilot. Green's aim was to do what no other person had ever done before on land. Fifty years before, United States Air Force pilot Chuck Yeager had flown faster than the speed of sound. Now, Green was going to attempt to break the sound barrier, too, but he wasn't going to be in a plane. He was going to be driving a car on land.

Green became the first person to travel faster than the speed of sound on land on October 15, 1997. He reached a speed of 763 miles per hour. What did Green say when one excited reporter asked him what the world looked like from the inside of a car going faster than the speed of sound? Green said, "The same as **stationary**, only faster."

Check Your Understanding

1. Which of the following answers does *not* mean the same as **stationary**?
   a. still
   b. fixed
   c. moving
   d. inactive

2. How were Green and Yeager alike?
   a. They were both pilots.
   b. They were both English.
   c. They were the same age.
   d. They were both racecar drivers.

3. The passage is mainly about
   a. what Green said to reporters.
   b. breaking the sound barrier on land.
   c. the straight lines marked out in Nevada.
   d. the first time the sound barrier was broken.

4. When was the sound barrier first broken?
   a. 1937
   b. 1947
   c. 1957
   d. 1967

/4

Warm-Up

14

Name _____

A Fighting Chance

Margaret Tobin Brown was in a lifeboat. The two crewmen were rowing as hard as they could. Though Brown and some of the other passengers were off their sinking ship, they weren't safe. They had to get far enough away from the sinking ship so that when it went under, they were not sucked under, too.

Brown was born into a life of poverty in 1867. She was wealthy now, but she knew her riches had come from luck and hard work. She knew the key to success was not giving up. Just because the luxury liner, the *Titanic*, had hit an iceberg and was sinking was no reason for **despair**.

Brown may have been a passenger, but she picked up an oar. She rowed until her hands bled. When one passenger began to say that they would never be found, Brown told him to "Keep it to yourself if you feel that way! We have a smooth sea and a fighting chance!"

Up until they were found, Brown wouldn't let the other passengers give up. She encouraged them to row so they would keep warm, and she shared her clothes. Many passengers died of exposure to the cold in other lifeboats, but everyone in Brown's boat survived. After Brown was rescued, she became known as the "Unsinkable Mollie Brown."

Check Your Understanding

1. When Brown says that they have a "fighting chance," she means that they will
   a. only survive if they are lucky.
   b. need to fight over who will row.
   c. have to start fighting over clothes.
   d. survive if they work hard and are lucky.

2. If you are in **despair**, you
   a. feel cold.
   b. feel lucky.
   c. feel exposed.
   d. feel hopeless.

3. One reason you know it is dangerously cold is because
   a. Brown picked up an oar.
   b. the *Titanic* was a luxury liner.
   c. there were icebergs in the water.
   d. the lifeboat could have been sucked under.

4. Which of the following answers is *not* true?
   a. Brown was born in 1867.
   b. Brown shared her clothes.
   c. Brown had always been wealthy.
   d. Brown encouraged other passengers to row.

/4

Warm-Up

15   A Walk Across the Ocean

Name _____

If you walk across water, you are usually walking across a bridge. In 1988, Remy Bricka walked across the Atlantic Ocean. How is that possible? Bricka lashed his feet to a pair of fourteen-foot fiberglass pontoons. He towed a raft behind him. The raft contained a sleeping compartment about the size of a coffin. In it, he stowed fishing tackle and three water desalinators. He also brought a sextant and compass for finding his way.

Bricka left from the Canary Islands on April 2. He averaged fifty miles a day. He ate fish and plankton that he scooped up from drifting schools. Two of Bricka's desalinators broke about halfway through his voyage. This would have caused many people to quit. Instead, Bricka just drank all the water he could **desalinate** plus a quart of seawater.

A Japanese trawler picked up Bricka on May 31. Bricka was near the island of Trinidad. He had hiked 3,502 miles across the open ocean. He was not in good shape. He was very thin. His weight had gone from 160 pounds to 110. He was also seeing things. His hallucinations were not pleasant. They were not of dry land or even drinking water. They were of trolls attacking his legs!

Check Your Understanding

1. Which of the following answers is true?
   a. Bricka left from Trinidad.
   b. Bricka was picked up on May 31, 1988.
   c. Bricka brought four water desalinators.
   d. Bricka walked across the Pacific Ocean.

2. When water is **desalinated**,
   a. salt is added.
   b. it is seawater.
   c. the salt is removed.
   d. it isn't safe for drinking.

3. For about how long did Bricka walk?
   a. ten days
   b. one month
   c. two months
   d. three months

4. If something is "packed away," it is
   a. towed.
   b. stowed.
   c. a sextant.
   d. a hallucination.

/4

Name _____

A Silent Discovery

In 1984, Katy Payne was at a zoo. She was sitting quietly, watching some baby elephants. Payne couldn't hear anything, but she could feel something. She described it as "a throbbing in the air and pressure on my chest."

Payne was an **acoustical** biologist. She had spent fifteen years studying the songs of humpback whales. She knew from her work that whales produced low-frequency sounds that people couldn't hear. She wondered if the elephants were somehow communicating like the whales did. Were the elephants using low-frequency sounds that people couldn't hear?

Payne brought a special tape recorder to the elephant pen. She found that its volume meter was picking up low-frequency sounds. The elephants were talking to each other! Payne went on to study wild elephants in Africa. She found that elephants can talk to each other across vast distances. How far apart can elephants be? They can be 186 miles away from each other and still talk! Payne points out that elephants can eat up to 500 pounds of plants a day. If they are too close, they will overgraze an area. Their language allows them to be apart but still talk. It allows them to coordinate their movements.

Check Your Understanding

1. **Acoustics** has to do with
   a. seeing or color.
   b. smelling or odor.
   c. feeling or touch.
   d. hearing or sound.

2. Most likely, Payne was able to notice the throbbing in the air because she
   a. could hear it.
   b. had been studying elephants in the wild.
   c. had been working with low-frequency sounds.
   d. was sitting far away from the baby elephants.

3. The passage is mainly about
   a. what Payne discovered.
   b. where Payne studied elephants.
   c. how Payne communicated with elephants.
   d. why Payne became an acoustical biologist.

4. How long did Payne study the songs of humpback whales?
   a. ten years
   b. fifteen years
   c. ten months
   d. fifteen months

/4

Name _____

Warm-Up 17 — The First to Summit

"Are you mad? We haven't a minute to lose. We must go down at once." These words were spoken by Louis Lachenal to Maurice Herzog on June 3, 1950. The two French climbers were standing on the top of Annapurna. They were the first people in the world to climb a peak over 26,247 feet. Annapurna is the 10th highest peak in the world. It is in the Himalayas in the country of Nepal.

The men had climbed without bottled oxygen. They had chosen to climb in their lighter boots as they dashed to the summit. Now, lack of oxygen, cold, and exhaustion were affecting Herzog's thinking. Yes, the two men had made it to the top, but success also meant getting back down alive. Lachenal started

swiftly down, but Herzog followed more slowly. At one point (he doesn't remember why), Herzog took off his gloves. As he saw them sliding down the slope, he remembers thinking that the consequences would be serious.

The descent took two weeks. The climbers' feet were badly frostbitten. Both climbers needed to have all their toes amputated. Herzog also ended up losing most of his fingers. Herzog never complained. He did say that if he had been thinking clearly, he would have used his spare pair of wool socks as a pair of gloves.

Check Your Understanding

1. Mount Everest is the highest mountain in the world. From the context of the passage, you can infer that
   a. Everest was first climbed after Annapurna.
   b. Everest was first climbed before Annapurna.
   c. Everest has been climbed without using bottled oxygen.
   d. both b and c are true.

2. From the context of the passage, you can infer that Herzog
   a. wanted bottled oxygen.
   b. could have saved his fingers.
   c. was a weaker climber than Lachenal.
   d. did not know the dangers of frostbite.

3. From the context of the passage, which of the following statements is *not* true?
   a. Annapurna is in Nepal.
   b. Annapurna is over 26,000 feet.
   c. Annapurna is in the Himalayas.
   d. Annapurna was first climbed in July.

4. *Descent* is to *go down* as
   a. *success* is to *fail*.
   b. *dash* is to *go slowly*.
   c. *amputate* is to *cut off*.
   d. *summit* is to *reach bottom*.

/4

Name _____

Searching Hot and Cold Deserts

Meenakshi Wadhwa was born in India. In fourth and fifth grade, she wasn't very good at math. She was scared of it. She didn't want to ask questions because she was afraid of looking stupid. It wasn't until she was brave enough to ask questions that she began to improve. Now Wadhwa studies and asks questions about Mars. She studies Mars by searching in hot and cold deserts. What is Wadhwa searching for and why in the desert?

Wadhwa is searching for meteorites. Meteorites fall all over the planet, but they are best found in deserts. This is because deserts have little vegetation. The lack of plant growth makes meteorites easy to spot. They are especially easy to spot in Antarctica. Their black color makes them stand out in the world of white.

How is it possible that some of Mars' crust can end up on Earth? Long ago, huge asteroids crashed into Mars. Bits of Mars' crust were knocked from their home planet and thrown into space. It is estimated that every day about fifty to one hundred tons of material from space fall into Earth's atmosphere. Most of the material is burned up. Martian meteorites are very rare because 99 percent of the meteorites that do make it through Earth's atmosphere are from asteroids.

Check Your Understanding

1. Most likely, meteorites from Mars are
   a. more likely to be in hot deserts than asteroid meteorites.
   b. not as black as asteroid meteorites.
   c. more common than asteroid meteorites.
   d. made of materials different from asteroid meteorites.

2. Why wouldn't Wadhwa ask questions?
   a. She didn't think she needed help.
   b. She was afraid of looking stupid.
   c. She was searching for meteorites.
   d. She was knocked by a huge asteroid.

3. If one hundred meteorites landed on Earth, about how many would be from asteroids?
   a. one
   b. fifty
   c. ninety-nine
   d. one hundred

4. Which of the following statements is true about deserts?
   a. Deserts can be hot or cold.
   b. Snow quickly melts in a desert.
   c. Most asteroids land in deserts.
   d. Vegetation cannot grow in a desert.

/4

Name _____

When the Fog Rolled In

When you think of bad weather, you may think of destructive hurricanes or twisting tornadoes. You may think of battering hail, blanketing snow, blistering heat, or the bone-chilling cold. You usually don't think of soft fog.

Jack Viorel loved to surf. He thought there was nothing better than riding waves. One day, he went with his surfing buddies to Ocean Beach in San Francisco, California. Ocean Beach is known for its big waves, strong currents, and the great white sharks that swim in its waters. All was fine until a fog rolled in. The thick, white fog was so dense that Viorel was blinded. He could not see the shore, lights, or his buddies.

Viorel called out over and over, but he became **disoriented**. He could not tell where the voices he was hearing were coming from. Soon, he couldn't hear voices at all. Viorel had to control his panic. He spotted a single light as the sun dipped below the horizon, but he didn't know if the light was on land or on a floating buoy. Viorel decided to paddle for the light. He paddled furiously, even when he was cold and exhausted and his arms felt like lead weights. Just when Viorel was sure he was going to collapse, a building came into focus. Fortunately, he had made the right choice.

Check Your Understanding

1. The author shows how bad weather can be in the form of fog
   a. by giving an example.
   b. by writing about sharks.
   c. by explaining what fog is.
   d. by talking about destruction.

2. When you are **disoriented**, you are
   a. dense.
   b. surfing.
   c. confused.
   d. exhausted.

3. Another title for the passage might be
   a. "Riding Big Waves."
   b. "A Fortunate Choice."
   c. "Surfing with Sharks."
   d. "Jack Viorel's Buddies."

4. Which of the following words best fit Jack Viorel?
   a. sloppy and lazy
   b. strong and angry
   c. hard of hearing and controlling
   d. adventure-seeking and determined

/4

Warm-Up
20

Name _____

The Lucky Flat Tire

The search was over. It was the end of the summer in 1990. The fossil hunters were ready to leave. First, a flat tire on their truck had to be fixed. All but one went into town while the tire was repaired. The one who stayed behind was a woman named Sue Hendrickson. While waiting for the others, Hendrickson decided to walk by some nearby cliffs. As she was walking along the cliff base, she discovered some small pieces of bone. Looking up at the cliff, she saw some larger bones **protruding** from the wall of the cliff.

What had Hendrickson discovered? She had found the most intact Tyrannosaurus Rex skeleton ever discovered! Eighty percent of the dinosaur's bones were there. Previously discovered T. Rex skeletons had, at most, 50 percent of their bones. The skeleton was named "Sue," after Hendrickson. What does Hendrickson say about the T. Rex named after her? She says she owes it all to a flat tire.

After discovering "Sue," Hendrickson went underwater. She explored a ship that was sunk while fighting pirates in 1600. She didn't find any dinosaurs on it, but she did find 400-year-old chicken eggs! What does Hendrickson say about her finds? She says, "Having it isn't what is thrilling; finding it is thrilling."

Check Your Understanding

1. From the context of the passage, you can infer that Hendrickson
   a. searched for different kinds of treasures.
   b. was mainly interested in dinosaur fossils.
   c. wanted the pirate ship to be named after her.
   d. liked working underwater better than on land.

2. Which of the following would Hendrickson find most thrilling?
   a. naming a fossil
   b. finding a fossil
   c. keeping a fossil
   d. looking for a fossil

3. When something **protrudes**, it
   a. sticks out.
   b. is very old.
   c. is due to luck.
   d. needs to be repaired.

4. Another title for the passage might be
   a. "The Lucky Chicken Fossil."
   b. "An Explorer's Discoveries."
   c. "The 400-Year-Old Skeleton."
   d. "The Woman Who Fought Pirates."

/4

Name _____

Warm-Up 21

The Boy Who Fed Cows

The winters in Wyoming are freezing. No matter how unbearably cold it was, Rulon Gardner had chores to do. Gardner's father was a dairy farmer, and two times a day, every day, no matter the weather, his cows had to be milked and fed. One of Gardner's jobs was to feed the cows hay. Each bale of hay weighed about one hundred pounds.

Gardner **participated** in sports in high school, but this doesn't mean Gardner skipped his chores. It just means he did them earlier or later. 365 days of the year, 730 times a year, Gardner picked up hay and fed it to the cows. All the hay lifting did something to Gardner. It made him very strong.

When Gardner was young, he could barely lift a bale of hay, but by the time he was a senior in high school, he could lift four bales of hay at a time.

The 2000 Summer Olympic Games were in Sydney, Australia. The Russian wrestler Alexander Karelin hadn't lost a match in thirteen years. Everyone expected Karelin to return home with yet another gold medal. As the world watched in shock, Karelin lost the gold medal to someone he had once beaten. He lost it to a farm boy whose strength had come from feeding cows!

Check Your Understanding

1. The lesson behind the passage might be
a. chores can be skipped.
b. hard work builds strength.
c. only people who lift hay get strong.
d. what you expect to happen will happen.

2. The passage does *not* tell you
a. what state Gardner lived in.
b. how many cows needed to be fed.
c. about how much a hay bale weighed.
d. how many bales Gardner could pick up.

3. If you **participate**, you
a. join in.
b. bale hay.
c. get strong.
d. lose a match.

4. From the context of the passage, you can infer that Gardner
a. liked cold weather.
b. moved to Sydney, Australia.
c. had wrestled Karelin before.
d. didn't have chores in high school.

/4

Warm-Up 22

Name _____

The Rhino with Glue-On Shoes

Lucy Spelman was a veterinarian. She needed to help Mohan, a captive rhinoceros. Mohan had infected feet, and it was painful for him to walk. Too often, Spelman had to drug Mohan and put him to sleep. This was always dangerous, as no one knew exactly how Mohan would react to the drugs. Then Spelman had to trim infected tissue from Mohan's feet.

Mohan weighed 5,000 pounds. He needed healthy feet to support all his weight. Spelman and the other vets tried everything. They even tried duct-taping bandages on his feet. Spelman finally figured out what was wrong. Mohan had worn down his toenails on hard ground. If Mohan had lived in the wild, he would have been walking on softer, muddier, swampy ground. As a result, Mohan was walking on his main footpad.

Spelman told another vet at the zoo what the problem was. Paul Anikis, the vet, came up with the solution. The solution was glue-on shoes! Anikis had used aluminum, glue-on shoes before on horses. After measuring Mohan's feet, special shoes were made for his back feet. Then they were glued onto his feet. Mohan wore three shoes on each foot (one for each toe). Both Mohan and the vets were happy with the shoes, as they greatly improved the rhinoceros's health.

Check Your Understanding

1. What might a zookeeper want to do to a rhino's cage?
a. make sure it is clean and dry
b. make the ground muddier and softer
c. make sure it is next to a cage with horses
d. make it small so the rhino doesn't have to walk

2. What were Mohan's shoes made out of?
a. tin
b. steel
c. plastic
d. aluminum

3. Most likely, when Mohan's shoes were put on, Spelman
a. had to drug Mohan.
b. had to cut them down to size.
c. first put them on with duct tape.
d. had no idea how much Mohan weighed.

4. How many shoes in total did Mohan wear on his back feet?
a. two
b. four
c. six
d. eight

/4

Warm-Up 23

Name _____

The Only Man with This Degree

When you go to college, you major in a subject. You may earn a degree in science, math, or English. It may be in art, education, or computers. There is one man who has a degree that no one else has. He is the only man in the world with this degree. What did this man major in? He majored in enigmatology. Who is this man? What in the world is enigmatology?

The man is Will Shortz. Shortz was born in 1952. He graduated from Indiana University in 1974. Shortz always liked puzzles, so he wrote his own major. An *enigma* is a puzzle, so an enigmatologist studies puzzles. Today, Shortz writes and edits puzzle books. He is also the puzzle editor for *The New York Times*

newspaper. He wrote the puzzle clues for the Riddler to leave for Batman in the movie *Batman Forever*.

What is one of Shortz's favorite crossword clues? The clue is, "It might turn into a different story." What is the answer? The answer is "spiral staircase." Shortz's favorite crossword puzzle ran on November 5, 1996. The puzzle had two correct solutions with the same set of clues. One of the clues said, "Lead story in tomorrow's newspaper." The answer was correct if you put in "Bob Dole Elected" or "Clinton Elected."

Check Your Understanding

1. An **enigma** is a
   a. clue.
   b. major.
   c. degree.
   d. puzzle.

2. Presidential elections take place on the Tuesday following the first Monday of November. From the context of the passage, you can infer that elections in 1996 were held on
   a. November 1
   b. November 3
   c. November 5
   d. November 7

3. The passage does *not* tell you
   a. when Shortz was born.
   b. where Shortz was born.
   c. when Shortz graduated.
   d. where Shortz went to school.

4. What might be the answer to the crossword clue "high home"?
   a. nest
   b. roof
   c. bell
   d. tail

/4

Warm-Up
24

Name _____

Six Months Inside

Shannon Lucid stayed inside for six months. Not once did she put a foot out the door. Not once did she open a window. She couldn't. This was because she was on the Russian space station *Mir* drifting 17,000 miles above Earth. The only other people on the station were two Russian cosmonauts.

Lucid had to learn how to live in zero gravity. She had to remember to be careful. Early on, she made a mistake. Lucid was doing an experiment with eggs. She accidentally released a few drops of a chemical into the air. It was only a few drops, but they split into a thousand tiny droplets. The droplets scattered across the module, or compartment, Lucid was working in. Instantly, Lucid hit the emergency warning button. The hatchway door slid shut. Pressurized cleaning gas pumped through the module as Lucid donned a facemask and breathing tank.

Despite Lucid's quick response, some of the droplets escaped the clean up. The after effects went on for days. All three of the space travelers suffered burns on their hands and arms when they touched a droplet. One droplet landed on a cosmonaut's cheek, just below his eye. The droplet burned and sizzled, leaving a permanent scar.

Check Your Understanding

1. An astronaut in Russia is called a
   a. cosmonaut.
   b. astrologer.
   c. astronomer.
   d. cosmetologist.

2. The passage is mainly about
   a. why people should stay inside.
   b. the benefits of living in space.
   c. an astronaut living in zero gravity.
   d. a space traveler with a permanent scar.

3. When you "put something on," you
   a. don it.
   b. burn it.
   c. touch it.
   d. sizzle it.

4. From the context of the passage, you can infer that Lucid
   a. made a lot of mistakes.
   b. didn't like experiments.
   c. had trained for emergencies.
   d. knew everything she needed to know.

/4

Warm-Up
25

Name _____

Attack of the Ants

Using a slingshot, Mark Moffett sent a fishing line into a tree. He then used the fishing line to pull a climbing rope over a branch. Next, he attached his climbing harness and wriggled upward. He was above the jungle floor in Peru when his support rope shifted.

Suddenly, Moffett fell several inches, and he began to swing. To make himself stable, Moffett flung a leg over a branch. That's when Moffett found himself attacked. He had smashed an ants' nest that was concealed by some plants living on the tree branch. Worker ants rushed out of the nest and covered his body. They bit through his skin with their mandibles, and they sprayed formic acid into his wounds.

Moffett was a biologist whose main focus was ants. Despite the fact that he became nauseated from the overdose of ant toxins in his blood from his many bites, Moffett had found something he had been looking for! He had found an "ant garden." An "ant garden" is when ants find and plant seeds. They plant the seeds in a papery carton the ants make out of chewed-up plant matter and soil. The plant roots then keep the carton from disintegrating in the rain. Moffett was impressed with his find, but he still pushed himself away to another tree branch!

Check Your Understanding

1. From the context of the passage, you can infer that some ant gardens are
  a. on the jungle floor.
  b. planted where it is very dry.
  c. on branches above the jungle floor.
  d. planted in places without many trees.

2. Most likely, Moffett shot a fishing line first because
  a. it was heavier than a climbing rope.
  b. it was thicker than a climbing rope.
  c. it was lighter than a climbing rope.
  d. it was stronger than a climbing rope.

3. Where was Moffett?
  a. Peru
  b. Poland
  c. Panama
  d. Paraguay

4. When something is "firm and steady," it is
  a. stable.
  b. nauseated.
  c. concealed.
  d. disintegrating.

/4

Warm-Up

26

Name _____

In Search of Glowing Dots

Karen Tejunga is over two hundred miles from the nearest road. She is in one of the wettest and wildest places on Earth. She is in Brazil. She is between two branches of the Amazon River on a lake that exists only during the wet season. It is a dark night, and she and her helper are all alone. Tejunga is a biologist. She is looking for caimans. The lake is a perfect place for these South American crocodiles to hide and attack.

As Tejunga swings her light, she spots several dozen pairs of glowing dots. The glowing dots are caiman eyes. Tejunga knows that if she falls into the water, any one of these nocturnal predators will eat her for dinner.

Despite this, Tejunga tries to get as close as she can. Her aim is to capture, measure, and tag the caimans. Radio collars will help Tejunga learn about the caimans' migration habits.

Tejunga uses a wire noose to snare the caiman's snout. The noose is attached to an eight-foot bamboo pole. Tejunga's helper will loop the caiman's tail with a rope once the wire around the snout is pulled tight. Once the creature is measured and tagged, it will be released.

Check Your Understanding

1. The glowing dots in the passage are
  a. eyes.
  b. teeth.
  c. tails.
  d. snouts.

2. A nocturnal animal
  a. is out at night.
  b. doesn't migrate.
  c. lives on dry land.
  d. is out during the day.

3. Using radio collars, Tejunga may learn
  a. what caimans eat.
  b. how caimans catch prey.
  c. why caimans have a long snout.
  d. where caimans go during the dry season.

4. The main point of the passage is to
  a. explain what a caiman is.
  b. discuss the Amazon River.
  c. list places that need roads.
  d. describe what one biologist does.

/4

Warm-Up 27

Name _____

At 3,000, He Stopped Counting

Trevor Thomas was on the Appalachian Trail. The Appalachian Trail stretches 2,175 miles from Georgia to Maine. Thomas's intent was to hike the entire trail. At one point, he met a fellow hiker. The two started talking about the trail ahead. The fellow hiker handed Thomas his trail book. That was when Thomas told him, "I can't read it. I'm blind."

Thomas became blind when he was an adult. He had to learn how to adapt to his new world, and he had to learn how to do things like use a cane and a talking computer program. Thomas said that hiking the Appalachian Trail gave him a goal. Thomas left on April 6, 2008. He was supposed to meet a friend at the Georgia trailhead.

The friend didn't show up so Thomas, with his fifty-pound pack and walking stick, started the long **trek** by himself.

Thomas hiked through roaring blizzards and blistering heat. He forded swollen, flooded streams. Thomas slipped and fell many times. Thomas stopped counting his falls when he hit 3,000. Thomas suffered broken ribs and hairline fractures. He chipped the bone in his hip. Despite his injuries, Thomas completed his trek on October 8. What did Thomas say about his journey? He said, "I proved to myself that although my world had changed, it wasn't becoming smaller."

Check Your Understanding

1. Which of the following words best describe Thomas?
   a. strong and clumsy
   b. courageous and weak
   c. determined and brave
   d. unfriendly and foolish

2. A **trek** is a
   a. short trip.
   b. chipped bone.
   c. journey, especially one on foot.
   d. hairline fracture.

3. About how long did it take Thomas to hike the trail?
   a. six weeks
   b. six months
   c. seven weeks
   d. seven months

4. What state was Thomas in when he finished his trek?
   a. Maine
   b. Georgia
   c. Virginia
   d. North Carolina

/4

Name _____

Saved by Charlie

Helen Thayer was the first woman to ski to the magnetic North Pole. Thayer braved brutal weather on her month-long **solo trip**. During one storm, Thayer's eyelashes froze solid. Then, her frozen eyelashes were snapped off by hurricane-force winds!

Despite the cruel and chilling conditions, Thayer could have survived the weather on her own. However, she could not have survived the polar bears. That's why Thayer brought along a husky dog named Charlie. Charlie was Thayer's polar bear alarm system. Charlie allowed Thayer to sleep at night, as he would alert her if a polar bear was near. Charlie pulled a sled that contained his own food.

One time, Thayer's way was blocked by a mountain of ice. As she turned to go around it, Charlie growled a loud warning. Thayer immediately tore off her skis, released her sled harness, and grabbed her rifle and flare gun. Suddenly, a bear appeared from around the mountain of ice and raced toward them. Rearing up on its hind legs, it dwarfed Thayer. Thayer released Charlie who grabbed the bear's right heel. The bear and Charlie went round and round as the bear tried to reach back and grab Charlie. Finally the bear tore loose from Charlie's grip and fled.

Check Your Understanding

1. A **solo trip** is
   a. one taken by himself or herself.
   b. one taken with one other person.
   c. one taken with a group of people.
   d. one taken with two other people.

2. What sentence gives an interesting but unnecessary detail to the main story idea?
   a. Charlie was Thayer's polar bear alarm system.
   b. Rearing up on its hind legs, it dwarfed Thayer.
   c. Charlie pulled a sled that contained his own food.
   d. Thayer released Charlie who grabbed the bear's right heel.

3. Another title for the passage might be
   a. "The Life of a Husky."
   b. "Where Polar Bears Live."
   c. "Blocked by a Mountain of Ice."
   d. "Thayer's Trip to the Magnetic North Pole."

4. What made Charlie a good polar bear alarm system?
   a. He could stay awake the entire night.
   b. He could sense a bear without seeing it.
   c. He could see a bear before Thayer could.
   d. He could immediately release his sled harness.

/4

Warm-Up 29

Name _____

In Pursuit of Whales

Paul Nicklen was in pursuit of bowhead whales. A photojournalist, Nicklen wanted to take pictures of the huge marine mammals. Nicklen was in a tiny boat all by himself. He knew the whales were close because he could hear them. He slowly motored along the ice edge until he spotted them in the distance. Wanting to sneak up on them, Nicklen went at a speed just above idle.

Nicklen continued along the ice edge when, all of a sudden, Nicklen was shocked to see a whale's head directly in front of him! A whale that was over five times the length of his boat was rising directly beneath him! Nicklen was trapped! Visibility was low, and the whale didn't see Nicklen at first. Nicklen quickly put his boat's engine in neutral. The whale's back was only one foot below him. The whale and Nicklen coasted along at the same speed.

Nicklen put his engine gently into reverse, but that scared the whale. The whale panicked and arched its back. The boat bounced off the whale's arched back as the whale's tail came up around the boat. Nicklen had to duck to avoid being hit, and then he had to bail out the 200-plus gallons of water that had splashed into the boat from the whale's tail!

Check Your Understanding

1. When you are "following something in order to catch up to it," you are
  a. in idle.
  b. in pursuit.
  c. in neutral.
  d. in reverse.

2. The passage is mainly about
  a. huge marine mammals.
  b. sailing a small boat.
  c. being trapped in the ice.
  d. a photojournalist's adventure.

3. How do you think Nicklen felt after his meeting with the whale?
  a. sad
  b. angry
  c. amazed
  d. confused

4. Why didn't the whale notice Nicklen sooner?
  a. Visibility was low.
  b. Nicklen was far away.
  c. Nicklen was motoring too fast.
  d. The whale's back was arched.

/4

Warm-Up **30**

Name _____

Another Way of Living

The dining room of the boarding house was on the fourth floor. When Cheri Blauwet wanted to eat there with all the other people her age, she had to be carried up by the maintenance man. When Cheri wanted to go places, she couldn't take the subway. She had to take expensive taxis. When she was by herself, she couldn't go on sidewalks. She had to go out in the busy streets.

Blauwet was in Argentina. She was doing a study **abroad** while in college. Blauwet was born in Iowa in 1980. She was run over by a tractor when she was one year old and lost the use of her legs. Blauwet could have done her study abroad in a country that was more wheelchair accessible. Instead, she went to a country where curbs prevented her from gaining access to sidewalks.

Blauwet said her experience was thrilling. She said it was challenging. She said that she was glad that she took the risk. Today, Blauwet is an accomplished athlete. She has won marathons and has competed at the Olympic level. Now a medical doctor, she works at educating people around the world that a mobility impairment and disability is not to be looked down upon or pitied. It is simply another way of living.

Check Your Understanding

1. If something can be gotten to or in, it is
   a. pitied.
   b. impaired.
   c. disabled.
   d. accessible.

2. Why didn't Blauwet go on sidewalks?
   a. She went the same speed as the cars.
   b. There weren't any sidewalks in Argentina.
   c. She couldn't get her wheelchair over the curbs.
   d. She liked the challenge of being on the street.

3. When you go **abroad**, you go to
   a. Argentina.
   b. a different country.
   c. compete in a marathon.
   d. an expensive dining room.

4. Most likely, how does Blauwet feel about being in a wheelchair?
   a. It's just the way she lives.
   b. People should feel sorry for her.
   c. It makes her so she can't take risks.
   d. It makes her not as good as other people.

/4

Answer Key

Answer Key

Interesting Places and Events

Page 9 Mystery of the Rolling Stones
1. b
2. d
3. a
4. c

Page 10 A Misnamed Ocean
1. b
2. c
3. d
4. a

Page 11 *Tet*
1. d
2. c
3. a
4. b

Page 12 A Massive Structure
1. a
2. d
3. b
4. c

Page 13 The Legend of Lady Carcas
1. d
2. d
3. b
4. d

Page 14 No International Postage
1. a
2. a
3. c
4. b

Page 15 Where the Unicorn Lives
1. b
2. b
3. a
4. a

Page 16 The Forbidden City
1. a
2. c
3. d
4. b

Page 17 The Tree in the Desert
1. b
2. d
3. a
4. c

Page 18 The Ice Bowl
1. b
2. c
3. d
4. a

Page 19 No Need to Build
1. d
2. a
3. d
4. a

Page 20 Needed: Hot and Cold Hands
1. d
2. d
3. c
4. a

Page 21 The Race Across the Sky
1. c
2. a
3. a
4. c

Page 22 The Giant's Causeway
1. b
2. d
3. c
4. d

Page 23 So Just Where Are You?
1. a
2. c
3. b
4. c

Page 24 Back on the Map
1. c
2. b
3. c
4. b

Page 25 The Case of the Poisoned Tiger
1. c
2. d
3. a
4. b

Page 26 Where Mud Blisters
1. c
2. a
3. d
4. b

Page 27 Squeaking Floors
1. d
2. d
3. a
4. a

Page 28 The Salt Is Always on the Table
1. a
2. a
3. d
4. c

Page 29 A City Instead of a Plant
1. c
2. c
3. a
4. b

Page 30 Tunnels in the Netherlands
1. a
2. b
3. c
4. d

Page 31 A Glowing Meal
1. b
2. d
3. c
4. a

Page 32 Where Are the Vikings?
1. a
2. a
3. c
4. d

Page 33 A Lake Impossible to Swim In
1. c
2. b
3. a
4. d

Page 34 The State Known for Syrup and Bridges
1. b
2. d
3. d
4. a

Page 35 Basketball Team Names
1. c
2. d
3. b
4. c

Page 36 Grasshoppers in Ice
1. d
2. b
3. c
4. a

Page 37 Hadrian's Wall
1. b
2. a
3. d
4. c

Page 38 Sleeping in a Capsule
1. a
2. c
3. d
4. a

Answer Key (cont.)

Scientifically Speaking

Page 41 A Weighty Puzzle
1. d
2. a
3. c
4. b

Page 42 A Living Dragon
1. b
2. b
3. a
4. d

Page 43 Pop Goes the Knuckle
1. a
2. c
3. d
4. a

Page 44 Lightning Strikes Twice
1. a
2. b
3. d
4. c

Page 45 Danger! Exploding Seeds!
1. c
2. b
3. d
4. a

Page 46 Lethal to Nonlethal
1. d
2. b
3. a
4. c

Page 47 An Animal Like a Raincoat
1. b
2. d
3. d
4. a

Page 48 One Plant, Two Cats
1. a
2. c
3. d
4. b

Page 49 What Could Be Humming?
1. c
2. a
3. b
4. d

Page 50 Into a Hurricane
1. a
2. c
3. c
4. a

Page 51 Positive Identification
1. b
2. a
3. d
4. c

Page 52 The Amazing Cat
1. c
2. d
3. a
4. b

Page 53 Invasion of Wings
1. c
2. a
3. b
4. d

Page 54 Strolling Across Venus
1. b
2. d
3. a
4. c

Page 55 All About the Jump
1. b
2. a
3. c
4. d

Page 56 What Cut Time?
1. d
2. b
3. c
4. a

Page 57 Bee Air Conditioning
1. b
2. c
3. d
4. a

Page 58 Yucky Breath
1. a
2. d
3. b
4. c

Page 59 The Strongest
1. a
2. c
3. b
4. d

Page 60 Robot Pills
1. b
2. b
3. d
4. a

Page 61 Surprise at the Necropsy
1. d
2. b
3. c
4. a

Page 62 The Disappearing Spoon
1. c
2. d
3. b
4. a

Page 63 Extreme Flying
1. c
2. b
3. d
4. c

Page 64 All About Nerves
1. d
2. a
3. b
4. c

Page 65 The Gutless Wonder
1. a
2. b
3. d
4. c

Page 66 Why the Scientist Knew
1. b
2. b
3. a
4. c

Page 67 Meat-Eating Caterpillars
1. c
2. d
3. c
4. b

Page 68 Motion Sickness
1. c
2. d
3. a
4. b

Page 69 An Impressive Crown
1. d
2. b
3. b
4. c

Page 70 Big Snakes
1. a
2. b
3. c
4. d

From the Past

Page 73 The Painting That Rode in an Ambulance
1. a
2. d
3. c
4. b

Answer Key (cont.)

Page 74 The Year Without a Summer
1. d
2. c
3. b
4. c

Page 75 Long-Ago Manners
1. d
2. d
3. b
4. b

Page 76 The Dog Who Came Home
1. b
2. d
3. c
4. a

Page 77 Left to Burn
1. d
2. a
3. b
4. c

Page 78 Uncle Sam
1. d
2. a
3. c
4. b

Page 79 An Engineering Masterpiece
1. b
2. d
3. c
4. a

Page 80 Seeing the Hidden Stomach
1. c
2. d
3. a
4. b

Page 81 The First Speed Trap
1. c
2. b
3. a
4. d

Page 82 First Play, Then Invention
1. d
2. d
3. b
4. b

Page 83 How Banneker Saved the Capital
1. a
2. c
3. d
4. a

Page 84 The Wall
1. c
2. b
3. a
4. d

Page 85 The Great Molasses Flood
1. c
2. a
3. d
4. b

Page 86 The Fruit That Wouldn't Sell
1. b
2. c
3. d
4. a

Page 87 The Trial
1. d
2. a
3. c
4. b

Page 88 Two Invitations
1. c
2. a
3. b
4. d

Page 89 Ship Numbers
1. a
2. a
3. c
4. d

Page 90 Second Only to Salt
1. b
2. c
3. a
4. d

Page 91 The First Skyscraper
1. b
2. d
3. c
4. b

Page 92 A Daring Rescue
1. b
2. a
3. d
4. c

Page 93 The Gold Miner's Diet
1. d
2. d
3. b
4. b

Page 94 The Man in the Mail
1. b
2. b
3. a
4. a

Page 95 Silk as Armor
1. c
2. d
3. c
4. d

Page 96 Why Sequoyah Wore a Turban
1. a
2. b
3. d
4. c

Page 97 Two Anecdotes
1. d
2. a
3. c
4. b

Page 98 Don't Be Late!
1. a
2. d
3. d
4. b

Page 99 Shopping Without Money
1. b
2. b
3. c
4. d

Page 100 The Hidden Medals
1. b
2. b
3. c
4. c

Page 101 Chained Shoes
1. a
2. b
3. a
4. b

Page 102 What Chipped China Led To
1. b
2. c
3. a
4. d

Did You Know?

Page 105 Dog in the Bathtub
1. a
2. c
3. d
4. b

Answer Key (cont.)

Page 106 A Boot That Is Not a Shoe
1. a
2. c
3. d
4. b

Page 107 When a Submarine Was an Iron Fish
1. b
2. c
3. a
4. d

Page 108 The State Bird That Isn't
1. d
2. b
3. a
4. a

Page 109 Fallacies
1. c
2. c
3. a
4. d

Page 110 Air Force One
1. d
2. b
3. c
4. a

Page 111 Painted Food
1. c
2. c
3. b
4. d

Page 112 When Ghoti = Fish
1. d
2. b
3. d
4. b

Page 113 What the Folding Chair Became
1. c
2. b
3. a
4. d

Page 114 Undercover Zookeepers
1. c
2. a
3. c
4. b

Page 115 Fire Dogs
1. d
2. a
3. b
4. c

Page 116 Gum in the Museum
1. c
2. d
3. b
4. a

Page 117 Athletes Wearing Plastic Bottles
1. a
2. b
3. c
4. d

Page 118 Ludicrous Laws
1. a
2. c
3. d
4. b

Page 119 If You Meet the Queen
1. d
2. b
3. c
4. a

Page 120 A Snake for Healing
1. a
2. d
3. b
4. c

Page 121 Why Round?
1. c
2. d
3. d
4. c

Page 122 Who Is Calling?
1. c
2. c
3. b
4. b

Page 123 The Black Box
1. c
2. d
3. b
4. b

Page 124 Memory Tricks
1. a
2. b
3. d
4. c

Page 125 The Nut That Must Be Shelled
1. d
2. c
3. b
4. a

Page 126 The Story Behind the Bug
1. d
2. c
3. b
4. a

Page 127 Setting Records
1. c
2. a
3. b
4. d

Page 128 Duct Tape
1. d
2. b
3. b
4. d

Page 129 What the Appraisers Knew
1. d
2. c
3. d
4. c

Page 130 Seen from the Moon
1. d
2. a
3. b
4. c

Page 131 The First Coin with Braille
1. c
2. d
3. a
4. b

Page 132 Do You Know Chameleons?
1. c
2. a
3. b
4. d

Page 133 Uluru
1. b
2. c
3. a
4. d

Page 134 The Mummy's Passport
1. a
2. c
3. b
4. d

Answer Key *(cont.)*

Fascinating People

Page 137 Running Around the World

1. c
2. a
3. b
4. c

Page 138 Nurse on Board

1. c
2. a
3. b
4. d

Page 139 Fire!

1. b
2. d
3. c
4. d

Page 140 Why a New Grove

1. d
2. b
3. a
4. c

Page 141 A Mystery Solved

1. b
2. a
3. c
4. b

Page 142 Shark Lady

1. c
2. d
3. d
4. a

Page 143 Just Water

1. b
2. a
3. a
4. d

Page 144 A Sticky Lesson

1. c
2. a
3. b
4. d

Page 145 A Fast Descent

1. b
2. b
3. c
4. a

Page 146 A River Test

1. a
2. a
3. d
4. b

Page 147 What to Say

1. b
2. a
3. c
4. d

Page 148 The Windsock That Dangled

1. a
2. a
3. d
4. d

Page 149 Only Faster

1. c
2. a
3. b
4. b

Page 150 A Fighting Chance

1. d
2. d
3. c
4. c

Page 151 A Walk Across the Ocean

1. b
2. c
3. c
4. b

Page 152 A Silent Discovery

1. d
2. c
3. a
4. b

Page 153 The First to Summit

1. a
2. b
3. d
4. c

Page 154 Searching Hot and Cold Deserts

1. d
2. b
3. c
4. a

Page 155 When the Fog Rolled In

1. a
2. c
3. b
4. d

Page 156 The Lucky Flat Tire

1. a
2. b
3. a
4. b

Page 157 The Boy Who Fed Cows

1. b
2. b
3. a
4. c

Page 158 The Rhino with Glue-On Shoes

1. b
2. d
3. a
4. c

Page 159 The Only Man with This Degree

1. d
2. c
3. b
4. a

Page 160 Six Months Inside

1. a
2. c
3. a
4. c

Page 161 Attack of the Ants

1. c
2. c
3. a
4. a

Page 162 In Search of Glowing Dots

1. a
2. a
3. d
4. d

Page 163 At 3,000, He Stopped Counting

1. c
2. c
3. b
4. a

Page 164 Saved by Charlie

1. a
2. c
3. d
4. b

Page 165 In Pursuit of Whales

1. b
2. d
3. c
4. a

Page 166 Another Way of Living

1. d
2. c
3. b
4. a

Self-Monitoring Reading Strategies

Use these steps with your students so they can monitor their own reading comprehension. Be sure to go over each step with the class. Distribute a copy to each student or enlarge to make a class poster.

✏ Step 1: Do I Understand?

Read a paragraph. Then ask, "Do I totally understand everything in this paragraph?" Use a pencil to mark a light **X** next to each paragraph that you comprehend and a light question mark next to each paragraph that contains anything you do not understand.

✏ Step 2: What Have I Just Read?

At the end of each paragraph, stop and summarize silently to yourself, in your own words, what you have read. You may look back at the text during this activity.

✏ Step 3: Does It Make Sense Now?

Finish reading the passage. Return to each paragraph that has a penciled question mark next to it and reread it. Does it make sense now? If so, great! If not, move on to step 4.

✏ Step 4: Why Am I Having This Trouble?

Pinpoint the problem. Is the difficulty to do with unfamiliar words or concepts? Is the sentence structure too complex? Is it because you know little background information about the topic? It's important that you identify the specific stumbling block(s) before you move on to step 5.

✏ Step 5: Where Can I Get Help?

Try a variety of aids to help you understand the text: the Internet, glossary, appendix, dictionary, thesaurus, encyclopedia, chapter summary, etc. Depending on what you are reading, use the resource(s) that will help you the most. If confusion remains after going through these five steps, ask a classmate or teacher for assistance.

As students become more comfortable with this strategy, you may want to make a rule that the students cannot ask for help from you unless they can do the following:

- identify the exact source of their confusion

- describe the steps they've already taken on their own to resolve the problem

Leveling Chart

Page #	Flesch-Kincaid Grade Level	Page #	Flesch-Kincaid Grade Level	Page #	Flesch-Kincaid Grade Level
Interesting Places and Events		**Scientifically Speaking** (cont.)		**Did You Know?** (cont.)	
9	5.5	62	5.4	116	5.8
10	5.6	63	5.3	117	5.1
11	5.5	64	5.1	118	5.1
12	5.2	65	5.0	119	5.3
13	5.7	66	5.6	120	5.6
14	5.9	67	5.3	121	5.6
15	5.8	68	5.4	122	5.3
16	5.5	69	5.8	123	5.3
17	5.0	70	5.3	124	5.7
18	5.1	**From the Past**		125	5.1
19	5.5	73	5.8	126	5.3
20	5.1	74	5.6	127	5.3
21	6.0	75	5.6	128	6.0
22	5.9	76	5.6	129	5.5
23	5.0	77	5.8	130	5.5
24	5.6	78	5.0	131	5.2
25	5.0	79	5.1	132	5.7
26	5.6	80	5.4	133	5.3
27	5.5	81	5.4	134	5.9
28	5.1	82	5.2	**Fascinating People**	
29	5.3	83	5.4	137	5.5
30	5.7	84	5.3	138	5.0
31	5.5	85	5.0	139	5.3
32	5.2	86	5.6	140	5.1
33	5.2	87	5.6	141	5.8
34	5.2	88	6.0	142	5.1
35	5.5	89	5.9	143	5.4
36	5.2	90	5.1	144	5.7
37	5.3	91	5.9	145	5.0
38	5.5	92	5.1	146	5.6
Scientifically Speaking		93	5.6	147	5.0
41	5.0	94	5.2	148	5.8
42	5.4	95	5.0	149	4.7
43	5.0	96	5.9	150	5.4
44	5.2	97	5.5	151	5.4
45	5.1	98	5.5	152	5.7
46	5.8	99	5.8	153	5.1
47	5.3	100	5.2	154	5.6
48	5.9	101	5.0	155	5.1
49	5.2	102	5.7	156	5.2
50	5.4	**Did You Know?**		157	5.6
51	6.0	105	5.2	158	5.3
52	5.5	106	5.4	159	5.3
53	5.6	107	5.4	160	5.4
54	5.3	108	5.8	161	5.4
55	5.3	109	5.0	162	5.4
56	5.4	110	5.6	163	5.1
57	5.4	111	5.1	164	5.3
58	5.6	112	3.4	165	5.1
59	5.8	113	5.7	166	5.6
60	5.8	114	6.0		
61	5.7	115	5.8		

Tracking Sheet

Interesting Places and Events		Scientifically Speaking		From the Past		Did You Know?		Fascinating People	
Page 9		Page 41		Page 73		Page 105		Page 137	
Page 10		Page 42		Page 74		Page 106		Page 138	
Page 11		Page 43		Page 75		Page 107		Page 139	
Page 12		Page 44		Page 76		Page 108		Page 140	
Page 13		Page 45		Page 77		Page 109		Page 141	
Page 14		Page 46		Page 78		Page 110		Page 142	
Page 15		Page 47		Page 79		Page 111		Page 143	
Page 16		Page 48		Page 80		Page 112		Page 144	
Page 17		Page 49		Page 81		Page 113		Page 145	
Page 18		Page 50		Page 82		Page 114		Page 146	
Page 19		Page 51		Page 83		Page 115		Page 147	
Page 20		Page 52		Page 84		Page 116		Page 148	
Page 21		Page 53		Page 85		Page 117		Page 149	
Page 22		Page 54		Page 86		Page 118		Page 150	
Page 23		Page 55		Page 87		Page 119		Page 151	
Page 24		Page 56		Page 88		Page 120		Page 152	
Page 25		Page 57		Page 89		Page 121		Page 153	
Page 26		Page 58		Page 90		Page 122		Page 154	
Page 27		Page 59		Page 91		Page 123		Page 155	
Page 28		Page 60		Page 92		Page 124		Page 156	
Page 29		Page 61		Page 93		Page 125		Page 157	
Page 30		Page 62		Page 94		Page 126		Page 158	
Page 31		Page 63		Page 95		Page 127		Page 159	
Page 32		Page 64		Page 96		Page 128		Page 160	
Page 33		Page 65		Page 97		Page 129		Page 161	
Page 34		Page 66		Page 98		Page 130		Page 162	
Page 35		Page 67		Page 99		Page 131		Page 163	
Page 36		Page 68		Page 100		Page 132		Page 164	
Page 37		Page 69		Page 101		Page 133		Page 165	
Page 38		Page 70		Page 102		Page 134		Page 166	